KU-699-691

Contents

Acknowledgements

For permission to publish the plays in this volume, the editor and publishers are grateful to the following authors and their agents: Bill Tidy, A.P. Watt (26/28 Bedford Row, London WC1R 4HL), John Junkin, Artistes Representatives (18/20 York Buildings, Adelphi, London WC2N 6JU) and the BBC for *The Fosdyke Saga* Episodes 1 and 2; Berlie Doherty and the BBC for *A Case for Probation*; Michael McStay, Bill McLean (23b Deodar Road, Putney, London SW15 2NP) and Central Independent Television plc for *Grandma Goes West*; Angus Graham-Campbell and the BBC for *Cutting Loose*; and Valerie Windsor and the BBC for *A Fairy Tale for Freudians*.

Any applications to perform any of the works, amateur or professional, should be addressed to the agents or, for *A Case for Probation*, *Cutting Loose* and *A Fairy Tale for Freudians* via the publishers.

We are also grateful for permission to use the cartoons and photograph in this volume: Bill Tidy for episodes from *The Fosdyke Saga* © Bill Tidy on pages 24 and 38; and M. Howarth for *A Case for Probation* on page 52.

Introduction

For most people, a play is something to be watched on television. For many of course, it is still something that is seen in a theatre. Few immediately think in terms of radio as a provider of plays, yet in Britain (as in Germany, Canada and Australia) plays on radio attract comparatively huge audiences. As John Tydeman, assistant head of the BBC Radio Drama department, puts it: 'When you compare the millions of people who hear a radio play with the readership the same author would reach through a novel or the number of people who might see the play in a theatre, you realize just how important a medium radio is.'

Over 500 plays a year are broadcast by BBC Radio every year. At least half a million people listen to 'The Afternoon Play' and sometimes the audience is double that size. Plays are also broadcast in other 'slots' on Radio 4: for example, 'Saturday Night Theatre', 'The Monday Play' and 'Thirty Minute Theatre'. This last slot often features new writers: two thirds of its productions are by people who have never had a play performed before, anywhere.

The same BBC department also produces (usually more serious) plays for transmission on Radio 3; but there are other producers of radio drama. The *Fosdyke Saga* series was made by the BBC Light Entertainment department. Many plays are produced by BBC School Radio and by the World Service of the BBC. Among the independent radio companies,

Capital and Radio Clyde have both had admirable drama departments at one time or another. It does however remain a fact that drama is one of the most expensive forms of radio and it is not always an attractive proposition to a commercial company.

There is also a suspicion (ill-founded as it happens) that 'plays on the radio' are only for the elderly or middle-aged; that they are designed to be listened to 'only' by housewives doing the ironing or by those in bed with flu.

This collection is designed in part to counteract that impression and to demonstrate the variety of radio drama, ranging from the realistic to the fantastic – including types of plays that could not exist in any other medium. It is also offered in the conviction that radio scripts work exceptionally well in class. Because the radio writer has only dialogue with which to create plot, character, conflict and action, it means that his or her play can be 'realized' simply by being read aloud. It is hoped that many young students will find this an enjoyable and satisfying process and that, for those who have not yet discovered radio drama, it will be a happy introduction.

The Fosdyke Saga

The Fosdyke Saga was created by the artist Bill Tidy as a strip cartoon for the *Daily Mirror* colour magazine. In fact it appeared as a daily serial in the newspaper itself, beginning in 1971. With playwright Alan Plater, Tidy adapted it for the stage in 1977. A great success, it was followed by *Fosdyke II* the next year. (Your editor was sitting in the front row of the audience at the tiny Bush Theatre in west London on its first night. He vividly remembers being given a piece of tripe to hold for much of the evening.)

The radio version, the first two episodes of which are included in this collection, was a collaboration between Bill Tidy and the comedy actor and writer, John Junkin. This was a completely new dramatization of the original cartoon strips and fully exploited the medium of radio. It was produced with a fascinating mixture of subtlety and panache by Alan Nixon, the over-the-top melodrama being decorated by surreal sound effects (see page 20) and tremulous cornet solos.

The saga begins in the period before World War I. It is set in the (imaginary) northern hell that is Griddlesbury where the much-oppressed Fosdyke family live at 14, Insanitary Cottages. 'Jos' Fosdyke works down the mine, much to the annoyance of his mates as he is supposed to be on strike. Eventually the family sets out for a new life, down south in Manchester. Up in Griddlesbury, Manchester is famed for its wealth. The Fosdykes have heard its streets are paved with meat pies and that there is even one house with a bath. It is on their journey there that they meet the Lancashire Tripe King, Ben Ditchley – and so the saga develops.

It has been criticized in some puritanical political circles as being reactionary and anti-feminist. It is of course simply a series of irrelevant jokes but (as the critic Gillian Reynolds has pointed out), it is also 'the good old humour of confounded expectation': you suppose one thing to be happening when something else (and usually something worse) is taking place.

It is also a parody and exaggeration of all the conventional images and stereotypes of northern life: incredibly poor and honest workmen and ruthless factory owners, all living on a diet of black puddings and, of course, tripe. Though *The Fosdyke Saga* leaves no cliché unstoned, it is richly inventive and, given a straight-faced, spirited reading, very funny.

A Case for Probation

With *A Case for Probation* we move firmly from the cartoon world of Bill Tidy's invention to the realism of Berlie Doherty's exploration of urban and family tensions.

It is set on Merseyside, where various attempts have been made over the years to overcome the problems of poor housing and inner-city decay. For example, in the early fifties, new estates were built on the outskirts of the city at places such as Kirkby and later (even further out) in new towns like Skelmersdale.

A Case for Probation shows how a move to a new suburb can signal an exciting new start for some members of a family while, for others, it means a painful break with the familiar and the loved. Interestingly, in this play, it is a younger member of the family who resents the move – not least because it will mean living at the wrong end of a lengthy bus ride from friends and entertainment.

The play is also about family relationships and shows what happens when one member of a family fails to sympathize with the hopes or anxieties of another. The characters are not divided into 'goodies' and 'baddies' in any way; indeed, in many ways this is a caring family. We are however asked to see the problem from one particular character's point of view. To this end, the play uses radio's ability (shared with the novel) to allow us to enter the mind of that character and to hear her thoughts as well as her spoken remarks. *A Case for Probation* is both an absorbing short play and a springboard for much discussion.

Grandma Goes West

You may have heard the perfectly true story of the man whose red Mini car was squashed flat when he parked it near a circus tent. It was sat on by an elephant trained to sit on small, round tubs.

There is another equally true story which actually happened to a couple who used to be neighbours of a cousin of the editor of this book. This man and his wife had been touring the continent with their car and caravan. Having stayed too long in southern Europe, they had to drive hard to reach the English Channel in time for the ferry on which they were booked. They took it in turns to drive while the other slept (illegally) in the caravan. During the small hours of the night, the husband felt the call of nature, stopped in a lay-by and disappeared behind a convenient bush. Meanwhile, his wife woke up and, wondering why they were not moving, got out of the caravan – dressed only in a flimsy nightie. As she looked for her husband, he returned and, without seeing her, got back in the car and drove on as fast as he could towards the Channel. . . .

Then there was the woman whose handbag, containing her driving licence, money and keys was stolen. The next day she received a phone call from a shop, saying it had been found on a counter. Would she come and collect it, the voice said. When she went to the shop, they disclaimed all knowledge of the call. The woman returned home to discover her house had been burgled.

'It's true . . . It happened to a friend' is both the usual introduction to such stories and the title of a collection of them (by Rodney Dale, published by Duckworth). They are sometimes known as 'modern myths' or 'urban legends', are often grotesque or macabre – and have always 'really' happened, though not to the teller of the tale. They have their variations. There are, for example, many versions of the story of the vanishing hitchhiker, the girl with the beehive hairdo, the poodle and the microwave and, of course, the granny on the roofrack.

In one version of this story, a family is on holiday in Spain. Granny, whom they have taken with them, dies while they are there. No one speaks the language. Rather than cope with the Spanish officials, they decide to drive home at once. The children refuse to have the body in the back of the car, so father wraps it in a tarpaulin and ties it on the roofrack. They negotiate the first set of customs with no difficulty and stop at the next café for a drink to celebrate the success of the plan. While they are in the café, the car is stolen.

In *Grandma Goes West*, Michael McStay has taken this

well-known example of modern folklore and turned it into a hilarious radio play which has the happy knack of making the listener or reader picture the action in vivid detail. However, he also has provided a realistic twist to its tail.

Cutting Loose
Angus Graham-Campbell's absorbing and convincing play illustrates a situation known to many teenagers: the question of whether or not to go on the family holiday.

Steve is under pressure to accompany two friends on their motorbike holiday on the continent for a month of 'sun, camping and women'. Not only will he be seen as 'weak' if he does not go, but his friends will be all the harder pressed financially as the plan is for him to go on the back of one of their bikes and to share the cost of the petrol. Meanwhile his parents assume that he will be coming with them on their usual Scottish holiday, and staying with his aunt. Even so, Steve has no real wish to disappoint them.

Cutting Loose follows the course of his conflicting loyalties and wishes, and then the unexpected and contrasting courses of the two holidays. Again it is a play which uses radio's ability to move swiftly from one location to another and to allow the listener to enter the minds of its characters. Interestingly though, in this play we are allowed to see things from Steve's perspective, yet are often distanced from him.

It is a play which reads easily in the classroom but is still highly dramatic. It is also a powerful motivation to group and class discussion.

A Fairy Tale for Freudians
A Freudian is one who accepts the teachings of the Austrian, Sigmund Freud. Freud is chiefly remembered as the founder of psychoanalysis which is a way of helping people who suffer from worry and nervous complaints. In psychoanalysis, they are helped to recall anxieties from their unconscious mind. Freud believed that many such anxieties are sexual in origin.

The word 'Freudian' is now used informally to describe anything to do with sexual ideas that lie within the mind without being expressed, while a 'Freudian slip' is a remark made accidentally and unintentionally but which shows what the speaker really means. Just why the last play in this anthology should be called *A Fairy Tale for Freudians* may prove a lively discussion point. Note the storyteller's final comment: 'Freudians may conceivably find some sort of meaning in all this.'

Others might call it 'A Fairy Tale for Feminists', seeing it as a satire on the way male chauvinists and, especially, the male chauvinists who dominate traditional fairy tales all view the world. Feminists will find it all too credible and realistic. They will also find its ending to be both tragic and predictable.

Seen purely as drama, its ending is of course delightfully unpredictable. The play also makes cheerful fun of many of the conventions and devices of fairy tales: repetitive plots, unlikely names, dreadful dungeons, magic swords, frog princes and pricking fingers.

Valerie Windsor's play is the story of a princess who refuses to be 'only' a princess. Princess Flora wants to inherit the kingdom, have a sword (like a prince) and go fighting dragons. A sophisticated play, it repays proper rehearsal.

Durations
The durations of the plays as broadcast will give an approximate indication of how long each play may take to read in class:

The Fosdyke Saga	15 minutes per episode
A Case for Probation	20 minutes
Grandma Goes West	30 minutes
Cutting Loose	30 minutes
A Fairy Tale for Freudians	15 minutes

The Writers

Michael McStay

Back in the 1960s, one of the most successful crime series was *No Hiding Place* starring Raymond Francis, Johnny Briggs and Michael McStay. Raymond Francis has gone on to appear in numerous productions, Johnny Briggs has found fame as Mike Baldwin in *Coronation Street* and Michael McStay has combined acting and writing.

After leaving *No Hiding Place* in 1966, Michael has certainly enjoyed a varied career. He appeared in 20 episodes of *Crossroads* ('I was brought in to woo Meg'), he produced a television documentary called *Operation Skua* about World War II and, in the last four years, he has turned his hand to writing.

'I'm fortunate that I'm able to see a lot of humour in even the grimmest situations' says Michael. 'For example, an entire episode in *Pull The Other One* is derived from the funeral of a friend of mine which I happened to find very funny. I haven't given up acting though. In fact, I recently recorded an episode of *Supergran* for Tyne Tees. Funnily enough, Michael Elphick has been in *Supergran* too. I think it must be the year of the Grandma with that and *Pull The Other One*.'

Angus Graham-Campbell

Born in Windsor, Angus Graham-Campbell read English at Cambridge (where he wrote his first play). He now teaches

English and drama and has written a number of successful stage and radio plays. Besides the theatre, his interests include travel and sport (he supports the Scottish football club, St Johnstone).

Of *Cutting Loose* he writes, 'I wanted to write a play about the difficulties and frustrations within a family when it comes to communication. I also wanted it to be about a young man's struggle for independence and the need for parents to listen and to realise the need for young people to break out from the family unit – and this does not necessarily entail irresponsibility and risk. Indeed, it is the frustrated Steve in *Cutting Loose* and not the more liberated Mike and Paul, who becomes increasingly at risk.'

Bill Tidy and John Junkin

Bill Tidy is himself a Northerner and a prolific and popular cartoonist who lives and works in Southport. Before that, his home was Liverpool. He claims to have spent one month in London but 'didn't like it'. He is best known for *The Fosdyke Saga* and also for *The Cloggies*, another Northern satirical strip which now appears in the magazine *The Listener*.

John Junkin started his career as a schoolteacher but turned to script-writing and, later, acting. He joined Joan Littlewood's 'Theatre Workshop' in 1960 and has appeared in a number of films, and frequently on radio and television, for which he has written or co-written many series.

Berlie Doherty

Berlie Doherty was born in Knotty Ash in Liverpool, spent her childhood across the Mersey on the Wirral, and now lives in Sheffield. She has written a number of books for children, had many short stories broadcast on radio and television and has had a number of plays produced on radio and in the theatre.

She says that the idea for *A Case for Probation* came from a real incident in Merseyside, when a new club was burnt out the night before it was due to open. 'In the play I tried to imagine why anybody would want to do a thing like that. When I go back to Liverpool, I hate to see what has happened to the close-knit communities that were like extended families. I don't forgive Carol for what she has done, but I try to give her and her parents a chance to speak to each other in the play.'

Valerie Windsor

Valerie Windsor started her career as an actress, but has done many different jobs including teaching. In the last five years she has been writing more or less full time. She has written several radio plays including *Variation on the Snow Queen* which won The Society of Authors/Pye Radio Award for the best radio play of 1981. She has also researched and written two dramatized features about the writers Winifred Holtby and Katherine Mansfield. She has also written for television and has just finished a novel.

Working on the scripts

In the classroom

The most informal classroom reading of a playscript is helped by rehearsal. Even a very experienced professional actor prefers to look over his part before a first reading in front of his colleagues. In the classroom therefore, those who will be reading should be given time to look over their lines: to make sure that they know when to pause, when to 'interrupt' the previous speech, and to work out the changing mood of their character before they are asked to read aloud.

It is much easier to read to a group from the front of a traditional classroom, and from a standing position or a position where you can be seen by your audience. It may be helpful to appoint a 'director' who will decide the location of various settings and rehearse the actors in basic movements, checking that they know when and where to enter and exit.

Note that it is possible for a group to break into smaller groups, and for each of these to rehearse its own interpretation of one or more scenes, and then present their versions in turn to the whole class.

Such an exercise can be an appropriate way of developing reading comprehension and of encouraging senstivity to a wide range of styles of spoken (and written) language natural to differing characters and situations and for varying 'audiences'.

Rehearsal and presentation of these scripts will also provide a basis for assessment of the various communication skills within the oral domain of GCSE English.

Tape-recording

An obvious way of presenting the radio plays in this collection is to record them on audio tape. The following points may be of help when recording:

(*a*)   Practise with your microphone to discover from how wide an angle it can pick up sound clearly.

(*b*)   Even the best microphone cannot produce a good recording over a long distance from the sound source. For speech, it should be 30–40 centimetres from the mouth. (Those readers with stronger voices can obviously be further away than those who do not project so well.)

(*c*)   It is much easier to record a play with actors standing rather than sitting. (They can easily tiptoe away when not involved in a dialogue, and so allow those who are speaking to stand in the best positions.)

(*d*)   Do not hold the script between mouth and microphone, and avoid rustling pages.

(*e*)   Rooms with bare walls produce a lot of echo. Unless an echo effect is required (for scenes set in a corridor or classroom, etc.) if possible use a carpeted, curtained room for recording.

(*f*)   Sound effects are important in any taped play. Don't worry about including every sound, but concentrate on those background noises which suggest location (for example, playground noises, bus interiors, etc.) and sounds which indicate the arrival or departure of a character. Avoid clumsy and accidentally comic sounds (like artificial footsteps) which can clutter or confuse the much more important dialogue.

(*g*)   Gently fading out the very last few words or sounds of a scene and fading in the first sounds of a new scene will suggest a transition from one scene to another, or the passing of time.

(*h*)   Several of the plays in this collection are particularly suitable for recording on location, especially as the necessary locations will be readily available. This will not remove the need for special sound effects, but these background noises will need some careful planning so as not to drown the dialogue.

In the radio studio
In the control room sits the director. With him is a senior studio manager who will supervise the sound balance of the microphones in the studio, the various sound effects and any incidental music. He does this on the 'mixing panel'. He can also produce such effects as an echo.

Also in the control room are one or two assistant studio managers who are responsible for playing the sound effects discs and music discs on the bank of record players, and also any previously recorded 'insert' tapes. Finally there is the producer's secretary who will keep a note of the timing of the various scenes.

Usually, the director will have an effects session with the studio managers before the actors arrive and will sort out which effects he wishes to use, how loud they will be, and so on. Any complicated 'mixes' of several effects may be recorded on tape, so that there is no need to keep on setting up lots of discs at each rehearsal. They may decide that some effects will be 'spot' effects, effects that will be created 'on the spot' in the studio. For example, it may be easier and more effective if an assistant studio manager or actor actually pours out a cup of tea near a microphone at the right moment in the play, rather than relying on a sound effects record being played from the control room.

Various microphones will be set up in the studio. One may be surrounded by screens covered in a soft material. This will provide a 'dead' acoustic that can be used for outdoor scenes.

Another microphone may be surrounded with hard screens that will create the slight echo of a semi-furnished room.

Also in the studio will be an 'effects door' with a variety of latches and bolts on it, and part of the studio floor may be covered with board. There may even be a gravel tray. These are so that the sound of footsteps on different surfaces can be simulated if the script requires them.

When the actors arrive, the director will supervise a 'read through' in the studio. He will then return to the control room and rehearse each scene with the effects. Besides hearing the actors and effects, he can see the actors through a window between the control room and the studio, and he can also speak to them on 'talkback' between scenes.

Sometimes a director will rehearse and then record each scene separately; sometimes he will rehearse the whole play before recording any of it.

Once the whole play is on tape, whether it is a radio or television play, and the director is satisfied he has all the 'takes' he requires, then the actors are no longer needed.

The last process is the editing together of the various scenes and then finally comes the editing of the play so that it is the right length for the slot it has been allocated.

Even in the professional studio it is sometimes necessary to resort to seemingly amateur devices, especially for out-of-the-ordinary sound effects.

A later episode of *The Fosdyke Saga* needed the sound of someone falling into a handcart full of tripe. The senior studio manager, Peter Harwood, solved the problem by using a sawn-off bicycle pump to make the whistling sound of the fall. For the 'impact', he recorded the noise of an upturned glass ashtray being plunged into a washing-up bowl full of papier mâché.

The background noise of the tripe factory was a mixture of sounds including old motor cars, bubbling porridge and twanging elastic bands.

The Fosdyke Saga

Episode 1

Bill Tidy and John Junkin

*First broadcast on BBC Radio 2 on 2 October 1983
(produced by Alan Nixon)*

Characters

Narrator
Josiah ('Jos') Fosdyke
Rebecca Fosdyke, his wife
Victoria ⎱
Albert ⎰ their children
Tom ⎰
Tod Openshaw, Rebecca's brother
Pimplejohn, his butler
Ben Ditchley, the Lancashire Tripe King
Roger Ditchley, his son
Pegleg Oldroyd
Official at the mine
Newsboy
Elsie, Mr Ditchley's maid
Members of the **crowd**

Episodes from The Fosdyke Saga *Cartoons by Bill Tidy*

The Fosdyke Saga
Episode 1

---

1   Narration

We hear the sound of a brass band.

Narrator: Lancashire, the turn of the century. At the heart of this grime-encrusted monument to the Industrial Revolution lies Griddlesbury with its cramped rows of miserable hovels huddled round Sweathorpes Colliery, only source of employment for the hungry masses of the town. Exploited by the mineowners the men slave in the stygian darkness while their women wait and worry at home. One such pursues her daily chores at number 14 Insanitary Cottages this fateful Friday . . . little knowing what lies in store for her.

2   The Fosdykes' home

In the distance we hear the warning hooter at the mine. In the house there is the clatter of crockery.

Victoria: [*Singing*] Oh God our help in ages past . . .

Rebecca: Hush, Victoria, is that the hooter at t'mine?

[*The singing stops and the house is silent*]

Victoria: I'll have a look.

[*She opens the window. The hooter sounds louder and a faint hubbub of voices is heard*]

Victoria: Ay, Mother, it's the alarm hooter . . .

Pegleg: [*In the distance*] Mrs Fosdyke . . . Victoria . . .

Victoria: It must be serious, Mother . . . Here comes Pegleg Oldroyd and he's running.

[*We hear a man with wooden leg approaching at a run*]

Pegleg: [*Sounding closer*] Mrs Fosdyke, come quickly.

[**The Fosdykes**' *door opens and the sound of running stops*]

Rebecca: Oh, Mr Oldroyd, wipe your foot and come in.

Pegleg: [*Breathlessly*] Mrs Fosdyke . . . there's been a cave in . . . No. 3 shaft . . . only one man down there when it happened.

Rebecca: It's Jos, I know it is!

Victoria: Father . . .

Pegleg: They're bringing him up now.

Rebecca: Victoria, get your shawl, we're going up there . . . not that one, your best one.

Victoria: It's not Sunday, mother.

Rebecca: No, but you might get knocked down on the way there . . .

3   At the mine

We hear the sounds of the mine at work but there is a general air of alarm and a loud hubbub of voices.

Rebecca: Let us through, let us through. Josiah! Jos, luv.

Official: Stand back, Mrs Fosdyke . . . give him air . . . he's badly shaken . . .

The crowd: [*General shushing*] ... Quiet... Order please ... Sssshhhh.

[*A total silence descends gradually*]

Official: [*Deliberately*] Can you hear me?

The crowd: Yes!!!

Official: I'm talking to *him*. Can you hear me, Jos?

Jos: [*Groaning*] I'll... I'll... be all... right. Give us a hand up.

Official: Can you walk?

Jos: Yes.

Official: Are you sure?

Jos: Yes, I can walk.

Official: Right. Then get walking – blackleg.

The crowd: [*Booing and hissing noises*]

4 The Fosdykes' home

We hear booing and hissing from the crowd outside the house.

The crowd: 'Strike now for twopence a week' 'Union solidarity' ... 'Blackleg'

[*We hear a cloth being wrung into bowl*]

Jos: [*Groans*]

Rebecca: Ah, that's looking much cleaner.

Jos: Rebecca, could you leave the windows for a minute and come and do summat to my head? Ouch! Go easy woman – eeh, what a mess, listen to that lot out there ... but I had to work through the strike to feed you and the kids. And look where it's got me. Nobody's speaking to me

... not a living soul, I've been sent to Coventry. What am I going to do, Rebecca? Rebecca?

Rebecca: Victoria, tell your father that as far as I'm concerned –

Jos: Oohh! Rebecca, it doesn't apply to you.

Rebecca: Oh, sorry Jos. Does that mean *I* can speak to you?

[*The mob outside is heard shouting again*]

Rebecca: [*Crying*] But this is driving me mad. We've got to get away.

Jos: Leave Griddlesbury?

Rebecca: We must, Jos. I don't want our children to have the kind of life we've had. Dust and danger and poverty. When that hooter went –

Jos: [*Interrupting*] Eeh lass, I suppose you're right. There's no future here for our Tom. Or Victoria ... or Albert.

Rebecca: Or Tim.

Jos: Or Tim. Eh? Who's Tim?

[*We hear a baby crying*]

Rebecca: I think it were the hooter up at mine that brought him on.

Jos: You mean ...

Rebecca: Yes, Jos. You've got another son.

Jos: One more mouth to feed! Well, that settles it. We're going.

Rebecca: Trouble is, how can we move without any brass? [*Wheedling*] Jos ...

Jos: I know what your're thinking, and I'm not going cap in hand to that brother of yours. I've got my pride. Nothing would make me grovel to him. Nothing!

[*A brick is thrown through the window. There is a cry of 'Blackleg' from the crowd*]

Jos: On the other hand ...

Rebecca: That's it, Jos. Swallow your pride. Put your Sunday best on and let's go and see our Tod now.

5 Rebecca's brother's house

We hear an expensive clock chime.

Tod: Looking for tick again, Rebecca? It's not much of a man that can't support his own family.

Rebecca: Tod, I beg you ... lend us the train fare to Manchester – we'll pay you back somehow.

Tod: Two shillings is a lot of brass, Beckie. But I'm not an unreasonable man. Children well?

Rebecca: Yes, thank God.

Tod: Good! I'll have my solicitors draw up a contract with them as security.

Jos: You'll not have my children as security, Tod Openshaw.

Tod: [*Laughing*] Fair enough, Fosdyke. Then there's another way.

[*We hear the tinkle of a coin on the floor*]

Tod: Here's a guinea. Grovel for it! [*He laughs*]

Jos: Never! Grovel at the feet of a fiend who exploits child labour in his sweat shop black pudding factory.

Tod: How dare you! Damn you! Pimplejohn!

Pimplejohn: You cursed, sir?

Tod: Throw these people out.

Pimplejohn: Yes, sir.

[*We hear sounds of scuffling with objects being knocked over. The door opens*]

Tod: [*Sailing over*] And let me tell you, Fosdyke ... Openshaw's black puddings are made with loving care and principally exported to be consumed by our brave lads fighting the Boers.

[*The scuffle ends as the family is thrown out of Openshaw's house. In the street we hear the distant cries of newspaper boys*]

Tod: [*Calling*] And while you're out there, Pimplejohn, get me a 'Griddlesbury Bugle and Clarion'.

Pimplejohn: Certainly sir. [*He calls*] Boy!

Newsboy: Yessir. [*He yells*] British eating cats and dogs in Mafeking!'

Tod: What! I'm ruined! Ruined!

Pimplejohn: Oh. In that case sir, will you accept this in lieu of two weeks' notice?

[**The butler** *throws a good hefty punch and we hear the shattering of a window*]

6   At the railway station

We hear the sound of distant shunting.

Rebecca: Well, Jos, we've sold what little we had, and with Tod's guinea which I secreted, there's enough to get us to Manchester.

Albert: We're going on a train! We're going on a train! Hey, what do they look like our Tom?

Tom: Look there, young Albert. That big ugly black thing puffing towards us.

Jos: Shut up son, that's the stationmaster. Here comes our train now.

[*A train slowly approaches and stops*]

Jos: Well Rebecca, it's goodbye to Griddlesbury and its dark satanic mills. And hello to Manchester where they say the streets are studded with meat pies, and I've heard there's one house with a bath.

[*We hear the hooting of the train's whistle and there is a puff of steam*]

Rebecca: Come on Jos, we don't want to miss it.

Jos: No, no luv. Not in there. It's a long journey, so just this once – as it's Tod's money, we're going to spoil ourselves and travel in style.

Rebecca: Oh Jos. You mean –

Jos: That's right luv. We're travelling – Pig class!

[*The train builds up steam. The couplings rattle and the train shudders as it moves off*]

Jos: And this is only the beginning!

7   On the train

The journey to Manchester has begun. We hear general sporadic coughing from the people in the carriage.

Tom: Father, they say that people in Manchester cough different. Is that true?

Jos: Ay, Tom lad. It is. People there have it easy. I've heard that some of them live well into their forties.

Rebecca: Give over, Jos. Stop filling the lad's head with nonsense.

[*We hear more coughing*]

Jos: Only another five and half hours Becky. Everything all right?

Rebecca: Well, I'm glad it'll soon be over. Little Tim is finding it hard to breathe under the accumulation of soot on his tiny face.

Ben Ditchley: Madam, would you care to wipe the infant's face with this?

Rebecca: Most kind of you, sir . . . but this is a piece of tripe.

Ben: [*Laughing*] Forgive me, I should have introduced myself. Ben Ditchley, the Lancashire Tripe King.

[*Their gasps of astonishment are drowned by the train's whistle*]

Jos: [*Aside*] Don't offend the gentleman, Becky. Wipe Tim's face with it.

[*We hear slurping noises and the baby starts screaming*]

Rebecca: I think he likes it, Mr Ditchley.

Ben: I could not help but overhear your conversation, sir. Are you seeking gainful employment of an honest nature?

Jos: I hope to improve my circumstances in Manchester, sir. Josiah Fosdyke is my name.

Ben: I like the look of you, Fosdyke. And your family. I'll tell you what I'll do. I'm willing to employ you at two shillings a week and all the tripe you can eat.

Jos: Done, Mr Ditchley. You'll not regret this day.

Victoria: [*Aside*] What luck, Mama.

Rebecca: [*Aside and sounding knowledgeable*] Not luck, Victoria. Mr Ditchley's searching glance noted your father's honest character, humility and good Christian upbringing. See how he's smiling at Papa, behind his newspaper.

Ben: [*His thoughts*] One searching glance was enough for me. You can always trust a man who tucks his shirt inside his underpants.

8 Manchester's railway station

The train arrives and we hear doors slamming as people disembark.

Ben: Right lad. Do you have anywhere to lay your head in town?

Jos: No sir, but we'll soon find a warm bridge to sleep under.

Ben: Nonsense! Come and stay with me and my son Roger till you find a hut. [*He calls*] Cabbie!

[*We hear a horse cab approaching*]

Rebecca: What a wonderful man, Jos.

Ben: The Slashings, Salford, please, Cabbie. Come on everybody.

[*The cab goes trotting off*]

Jos: He's a saint.

Rebecca: I hope his son won't resent us.

Jos: No luv, he's really taken to us. A job, a place to stay . . .

Rebecca: And he's letting us run behind his cab.

[*We hear the sound of trotting hooves fade into the distance*]

9 At Ben Ditchley's home

We hear the tinkling of crockery.

Jos: This is very kind of you, Mr Ditchley.

Ben: Not at all Fosdyke. A little refreshment after that long journey, then I'll show you where you're going to stay. More tea, Mrs Fosdyke?

Rebecca: Oh, thank you.

Ben: Elsie, attend to Mrs Fosdyke.

[*We hear tea being poured*]

Rebecca: No sugar this time, thank you.

Ben: There was no sugar last time.

Rebecca: Oh, it just tasted a little sweet.

Ben: Elsie, you're not washing those jam jars out proper.

[*There is an embarrassing silence*]

All: [*We hear nervous coughing, and then everyone starts to speak at once*]

[*We hear a door slam and voices mumbling in the distance; there is a scream from* **Elsie**]

Ben: Ah, that'll be Roger, my son. He's up from Oxford, you know. Studying Greek Philosophy and English philandering.

[*The door opens*]

Roger: Hello Pater. You're putting on weight. I think it's your wallet. Can you lend me twenty guineas?

Ben: Of course lad. Here, help yourself. Catch!

Roger: Ooof! Thanks Pater. Oh hello, who are you?

Victoria: Mmm ... ermm ...

Jos: Stand up girl ... straighten yourself up. Stick your chest out.

Roger: Mmm I say!

Jos: No, on second thoughts ... This is my daughter Victoria, Master Roger.

Ben: Sorry, Roger. These are the Fosdykes ... decent enough folk ... I'm taking him on at the works to replace old Frigley ... keeps dropping off ... well, bits of him do!

Roger: Oh jolly good. I'm sure if you work hard and diligently, in 40 or 50 years you'll be in the same state as old Frigley, what! Ha, ha. Well Pater, must be off now. Hope to see you again, Miss Victoria.

[*We hear the door opening and closing*]

Ben: 'Eee, that lad of mine. D'you know, he's been my one consolation since the late Mrs Ditchley went to the great tripe dresser in the sky.

Rebecca: Oh, Mr Ditchley ... did she suffer?

Ben: I don't know, Missus, I never thought to ask her. Well, no use dwelling in the past ... finished your tea? Right, I'll show you where you're going to stop. If you all follow me ...

10 In Mr Ditchley's garden

We hear a door catch closing and the sound of feet clumping on cobbles.

Jos: Oh, Mr Ditchley, I just don't know what to say.

Ben: Say nowt, Fosdyke. You and your family stay there as long as you like, till you find a place of your own.

Rebecca: But Mr Ditchley, won't it inconvenience you having us there?

Ben: Not a bit of it, my dear. Since we had the indoor one fitted we hardly ever use this!

Albert: Mam, I'm tired.

Victoria: Albert, hush, Mr Ditchley's speaking.

Ben: It's all right, luv, that run from the station carrying my suitcases must have tired the little . . . boy. You all look fair thrumped, I suggest you all get your heads down and I'll see you at the works tomorrow, Fosdyke.

Jos: Thank you Mr Ditchley. What time should I start?

Ben: Lad, we all start at the same time at Ditchleys . . . but, you've had a long hard journey . . . why don't you just stroll up at daybreak! G'night all.

[*We hear his departing footsteps*]

Jos: That man is a living saint.

11   At the Fosdykes' temporary home

We hear the door opening and the family entering.

Rebecca: Victoria, you over there. Tom, Albert in the corner, I'll put the baby here, he'll be safe enough with the lid down, your father and me'll go here, and we'll all take it in turns to lay down.

[*There is general grunting as the family settles down to sleep until all we hear is the sound of regular breathing*]

Rebecca: Are you awake, Jos?

Jos: I've got a headache, luv.

Jos: Jos, what a day it's been. Leaving Griddlesbury, meeting Mr Ditchley, the Lancashire Tripe King –

Jos: Me getting a job on our first day in Manchester. Ee, Becky, I think that the luck of the Fosdykes has finally taken a turn for the better.

The Fosdyke Saga
Episode 2
Bill Tidy and John Junkin

First broadcast on BBC Radio 2 on 9 October 1983
(produced by Alan Nixon)

Characters

Narrator
Josiah ('Jos') Fosdyke
Rebecca Fosdyke, his wife
Victoria, their daughter
Ben Ditchley, the Lancashire Tripe King
Roger Ditchley, his son
Boakes, an employee at the tripe works
Doctor
Mrs Scraunce, proprietor of the 'Duck and Weave'

Episodes from The Fosdyke Saga *Cartoons by Bill Tidy*

The Fosdyke Saga
Episode 2

---

1 Narration

Narrator: After shaking the grime of Griddlesbury off their
shoes, the Fosdyke family (Jos, Becky, their lovely
daughter Victoria, sons Tom and Albert and baby Tim) fall
on their feet through a fortuitous encounter with Ben
Ditchley the legendary Lancashire Tripe King who offers
them food and shelter and employment for Josiah. The
magnate's kindly eye falls upon the nubile Victoria and the
possibility of a union augurs well for the Fosdykes.
Dashing home to apprise his family of the good tidings,
Josiah is unaware that the magnate's son, Roger Ditchley
is at the moment bidding fair to become the fly in the
ointment of his joy.

2 At the tripe works

Boakes: ... This is the Scalding Shed where you'll be
starting Fosdyke. Every day summat like 2,000 belly of
crude tripe is treated by the unique Ditchley scalding and
priming process and emerges over there in the throping
chamber to be sized, grappled and defenestrated.

Jos: Yes, Mr Boakes, I think I understand.

Boakes: Never mind 'Yes Mr Boakes'. Just see that you do it. You might be a friend of old man Ditchley but I run the Scalding shed. I'll be keeping my eye on you.

Jos: You'll have no cause for complaint from me, Mr Boakes.

Boakes: We'll see, lad, there's a lot as don't survive the Scalding shed.

[*We hear a loud hiss of steam*]

3   At the tripe factory

Jos *has been busily working.*

Jos: Mr Boakes, I've plugged that leak in Walter's overalls, all the carboys are full and I've scoured out the reserve groting chamber in case you need it.

Boakes: By gum, Fosdyke, you're a goer. It took Frigley twelve year and two marriages to reach that level and then he started dropping to bits.

Ben: [*Approaching*] Ah, Boakes. How's he shaping up, Boakes?

Boakes: This man's got tripe in his blood Mr Ditchley. He's learned more in the last six months than old Frigley did in a lifetime, and not a bit dropped off him. He's conscientious, punctual, and doesn't bruise easy, and I've had no complaints from the girls in the Flensing shed about him.

Ben: That reminds me. I want a word with you, Fosdyke. Can I use your office, Boakes?

Boakes: Yes, sir.

4   At the tripe works: in Boakes' office

We hear the door open.

Ben: Well, don't stand there. Come in, this is private.

[*The door closes shutting out the sound of the tripeworks*]

Jos: I hope there's nowt wrong, Mr Ditchley?

Ben: No, lad, nothing. I just wanted a couple of words, man to man, rich man to poor man of course, ha ha ... it's er ... about that daughter of yours.

Jos: Our Victoria?

Ben: Aye.

Jos: She's not being a nuisance is she? I know she's round at your house regular but if she's getting in the way.

Ben: Ee lad, quite the contrary, I've become quite ... er ... fond of the lass.

Jos: Oh!

Ben: In fact ... well, I'm going to be frank with you, Fosdyke – May I call you ... Jos?

Jos: Of course, Mr Ditchley.

Ben: Well, Fosdyke, your Victoria is built like a drayhorse and since Mrs Ditchley passed on ... well, I'll be honest with you, there's nowt in my cold lonely bed in winter but me and some biscuit crumbs. Do you follow my meaning?

Jos: Well, I don't know, Mr Ditchley. Our Vicky is a nice respectable young girl –

Ben: No, no Fosdyke, I mean ... wedlock. I'm asking you to be my father-in-law!

Jos: But Mr Ditchley, she's only –

Ben: There's a partnership in it for you!

Jos: But you're old enough to be her –

Ben: And a seat on the West Lancs Tripe Foundation board!

Jos: But there's fifty years –

Ben: Membership of the exclusive Tripeneum Club and the Tripe Exchange. Why, that little lot is worth a fortune. What do you say?

Jos: [*After a pause*] Well, of course, there's three months between me and Becky and we've always been happy.

Ben: I knew you'd see reason ... Dad!

Jos: Ben –

Ben: Now, Fosdyke, the marriage has not been solemnized yet.

Jos: Sorry, Mr Ditchley. May I go and tell the family? Becky will be delighted, and I'm sure that this will make our Victoria the happiest girl in the world.

5   At the Duck and Weave

Victoria *and* **Roger** *have run away together.*

Victoria: Oh ... oh ... this has made me the happiest girl in the world.

Roger: I don't get many complaints. If you'll pass my herbal mixture from the bedside table, very shortly we can start all over again ...

6   At the Fosdykes' temporary home

Jos: Becky, Becky ... where are you?

Rebecca: Jos! We've only got one room. I'm here, behind this parish loaf. Now calm down, Jos, I've got something to tell you.

Jos: No, no Becky, my news first. Our Victoria's going to be . . .

Rebecca: I know, Jos . . . Mrs Ditchley. That's what I was going to tell you.

Jos: But, but . . . how did *you* know? I've only just finished talking to him.

Rebecca: Oh, did you see them before they left?

Jos: Left? Left?

Rebecca: Yes. I don't really approve of this running away, but as long as they're going to be married . . .

Jos: What's all this about running away? I've just left him in his office.

Rebecca: Office? Roger hasn't got an office.

Jos: Roger? What are you going on about him for? I'm telling you, our Victoria's going to marry Ben. Ben Ditchley.

Rebecca: But he's old enough to be her –

Jos: What does the age difference matter when I'm going to be a partner in the firm –

Rebecca: A partner?

Jos: Ay . . . and I'll have a seat on the West Lancs Tripe Board.

Rebecca: Yes but –

Jos: And membership of the exclusive Tripeneum Club, *and* the Tripe Exchange!

Rebecca: Well, I don't know . . .

Jos: Don't you understand, Becky? We're made. Made for life.

Rebecca: But what about Roger?

Jos: Old Ben's the one in charge, Becky. He makes the decisions. We can forget Roger.

Rebecca: I don't think we can, luv. Not just like that.

Jos: For pity's sake woman, why not?

Rebecca: He's just run off with our Victoria.

Jos: What?

Rebecca: They left this note.

[*We hear the paper rustling*]

Jos: [*Reading*] 'Dear Mama and Papa, Roger and I are in love and have gone away for a few days to settle our future. I am sure that next time you see me, I will be Mrs Roger Ditchley, Your loving daughter Victoria.' Augh . . .

Rebecca: Jos, are you all right?

Jos: Becky, I'm shocked. Deeply shocked and ashamed, to think that our daughter who we brought up to be a good girl, should, for a moment of passion risk losing her honour, our good name and my seat on the Tripe Board.

Rebecca: What are we going to do, Jos?

Jos: Let me think, woman . . . We've got to find them and bring them back before he finds out. They must have been seen. You get out and ask around, discreetly and I'll go and try to bluff the old man. And hurry woman, the whole future of the Fosdykes is at stake!

7 At the tripe works

Ben: Now get it sorted out Boakes. Two thousand ton of best honeycomb tripe gone missing between here and Blackbury, that's the fourth time this month . . . Tonight I want you to look under everyone's car before they leave.

[*There is a tentative knock*]

Ben: [*Angrily*]Come in!

[*The door opens*]

Ben: Ah, come in Fosdyke. On your way Boakes, and get it sorted out, or else.

[*The door closes*]

Ben: Sit down, Jos ... Eeehh it's been a bad morning. Some of these people are earning half a crown a week and they still steal from me. I'm surrounded by scoundrels and liars. If there's one thing I can't abide it's a liar. It's a delight to see your friendly honest face. Now, what news of my beloved?

Jos: [*Gulping nervously*] Well ... er ... well ...

Ben: What's up lad? She's all right, isn't she?

Jos: Oh yes ... yes ... well not exactly no.

Ben: You mean – she's ill?

Jos: No ... no ... well actually ... yes.

Ben: What's wrong with her?

Jos: It's her leg ... something she ate ... no ... er ...

Ben: Jos! Jos! You're avoiding the truth.

Jos: No, Mr Ditchley –

Ben: After 40 years in business I can spot a liar quicker than a rat can savage a blancmange. You're keeping something from me.

Jos: No, Mr Ditchley ...

Ben: Jos. The truth now ... what's up with Victoria? Don't be afraid to tell me. Wrinkled elbows, moles in unusual places ... speak up, and as long as you tell me the truth, I can take anything.

Jos: She's run away with your Roger.

Ben: [*He takes a strangled intake of breath*]

[*We hear a body falling off a chair onto a desk and onto the floor*]

8   At Mr Ditchley's home

We hear heavily laboured breathing.

Rebecca: How is he doctor?

Doctor: Well his breathing's improved. You can stay with him for a while, but whatever you do, don't upset or excite him until he's paid my bill.

Rebecca: Can he hear us, Doctor?

Doctor: Oh he's quite conscious, getting calm and more lucid all the time.

Ben: Get out you quack. You've killed more people in this town than the horseless carriage.

Doctor: With occasional lapses into delirium. I'll call back in the morning. Good day to you.

[*We hear the door open and close*]

Jos: I'm sorry Mr Ditchley . . . trying to lie to you like that. I only wanted to spare your feelings.

Ben: I know that, Jos, you showed a lot of tact for an ignorant working man. It's just that son of mine. [*Growing angry*] That ne'er do well, worthless scoundrel –

Rebecca: Don't get excited Mr Ditchley, you nearly knocked over your enema set.

Ben: My own flesh and blood . . . the seed of my loins stealing the lass I was going to wed.

Rebecca: Oh no, Mr Ditchley . . . it may be just an innocent outing for two young people.

Ben: Nay, nay . . . if I know bloody Roger he's put her up the stick by now.

Jos: Oh no, Mr Ditchley that cannot be.

Ben: [*Livid*] Are you saying my lad's not capable?

Jos: [*Strangulated*] No, no Mr Ditchley . . . aaaahh . . .

[*Sounding normal*] I'm sorry I got my throat caught up in your hands then.

Ben: Find them, Jos, find them. I've got my heart set on marrying Victoria. If you can get her back here discreetly, within 48 hours, I'm prepared to forgive and forget, as far as she's concerned, but as for that dastardly son of mine . . . [*He has a fit of coughing*]

Jos: [*Aside*] Come on Becky, it's our only chance, we've got to find them, wherever they are.

9   At the Duck and Weave

Roger: [*Yawning and drinking*]

Victoria   That's your second bottle of herbal mixture today Roger.

Roger: Oh shut up, woman. You're talking like a wife.

Victoria: [*Coyly*] Well, Roger, I soon will be one.

Roger: Really? Congratulations. Who's the lucky fellow?

Victoria: Oh Roger, your ready wit is much too fast for a simple girl like me. Do you think they will be looking for us?

Roger: Who cares? Now do be quiet and pass me that paper . . . I er . . . I want to do the crossword.

[*We hear the rustle of a newspaper*]

Victoria: Here you are dear. Is it a hard crossword in the 'White Slaver's Gazette'?

Roger: Hush, girl.

Victoria: I'm sure they will be looking for us . . . your father and mine . . .

Roger: [*Musing*] B.O.R.D.E.L.L.O. . . . Yeees . . .

Victoria: Darling, let's get married and then they can never part us.

Roger: So four across must be ... Thighs ...

Victoria: In fact, Roger ... we may *have to* get married ...

Roger: Six across ... 7 letters ... 'A significant pause' ... Err, first letter P.

Victoria: I'm expecting a baby.

Roger: P...R...E...G... Pregnant!!!!

Victoria: Yes. So you see, Roger, it would be for the best if we married soon.

Roger: I have not considered marriage at all. Heavens, you're only a working class strumpet and I am a gentleman of breeding.

Victoria: [*Weeping*] But Roger –

Roger: To me you are but a plaything. An object of pleasure. Something to be used and tossed aside.

Victoria: Roger, I sense that you have grown cold towards me.

Roger: No, not cold, Victoria ... you just ... *bore* me. Pass me my cravat.

Victoria: Roger, you're putting your clothes on! You're not leaving me?

Roger: Do you think you can saddle me with a mewling infant? No thanks. Goodbye, Victoria, you were a mildly amusing diversion.

[*We hear the door open*]

Victoria: Roger! You're not leaving – just like that?

Roger: No, Victoria, you're right. My honour as a gentleman ... I'll come back –

Victoria: Thank God!

Roger: For my walking stick and trousers . . . Goodbye.

[*We hear his footsteps receding down the stairs*]

Victoria: Roger! [*Sobbing*] What am I to do? Thrown aside at the whim of a heartless philanderer. I hate you, Roger Ditchley, I hate you, I hate you!

[*There is a knock on the door*]

Victoria: Roger, darling . . . you've come back to me. I fly to your arms. Kiss me my beloved –

[*The door opens*]

Victoria: Mrs Scraunce!

Mrs Scraunce: Your gentleman friend's hopped out without paying the rent . . . [*Sarky*] Mrs Smith. It's four quid or out you go.

Victoria: But . . . I have no money . . .

Mrs Scraunce: Then out you go! Pack your bags and be off with you.

Victoria: I have no bags . . . nothing.

Mrs Scraunce: Oh, one of them are you? Well you're not giving the Duck and Weave a bad name. Come along . . .

[*We hear sounds of shouting and crying as the pair noisily retreat down the stairs*]

Mrs Scraunce: Out on the streets, where you belong.

[*We hear the door slam. At the same time there is a peal of thunder and it begins to rain*]

Victoria: What's to become of me? I'm ruined. Ruined. I can never return to my family.

A Case for Probation
Berlie Doherty

*First broadcast on BBC School Radio on 14 May 1983
(produced by Peter Fozzard)*

Characters

Carol, a teenage girl
Mum
Dad

NB Groups reading this play may choose to cast the part of
Carol with two readers: one for the narrative passages and
another to read the dialogue.

Tracey Ullman records A Case for Probation *(M. Howarth)*

A Case for Probation

1 Narration

Carol: [*Narrating*] He asked me to write this down because he thought it might help to sort things out. I don't know if it will really, but I have such terrible dreams about it all – like a record that goes on and on playing, and every time I think I've got to the end it starts again. I talk to him about it, but he's the only one who understands. He's my probation officer. He's my friend.

[*We start to hear the noises of a street*]

Carol: [*Narrating*] It started just before we moved. We'd always lived in the terrace – Woodbine Terrace, Liverpool. My Mum had lived there, in the same house, with her brothers and sisters. We knew everyone in the terrace – as if we were all one big family. In a way, I suppose we were. We did everything out in the terrace – all the mums would take out their vegetables to peel and sit on the doorsteps in the sunshine gossiping away, and we'd all be playing out with our marbles and skateboards and hopscotch. Saturday mornings Zena and I would go off to the baths or the pictures, then stop in at the chippie on the way home and sit on the end wall eating them and laughing at the lads. We hadn't much money – my dad had been out of work for two years, but it didn't seem to matter all that much. 'We'll manage' – my mum always said. And we did.

[*We hear the noises of a kitchen*]

Carol: [*Narrating*] Then one day my dad came home from signing on. He strode into the kitchen like a young man.

2 The family's house: the kitchen

Dad: [*Shouting*] Carol, where's your mother? Fetch her, will yer? I've got something to tell her.

Carol: She's round at Ma Elliot's, feeding their twins. What's up Dad?

Dad: No, I'll not tell you till your mother's here. Run and fetch her. [*Shouts*] And tell her it's good news!

[*A short time later*]

Mum: [*Breathlessly*] It better had be an' all . . . that little fat one was sick all over me when our Carol run in like that.

Dad: Right love, well . . . I've two good things to tell yer. First . . . I'm fixed up with a job!

Mum: Oh John! There, I knew you'd be all right, love. I knew you'd do it!

Carol: About time too! You've been sniffing round the house like a dog that nobody wants to take for a walk for months on end.

Mum: That'll do Carol. No need to cheek your father. Well, and what's the next bit?

Dad: Wait till you hear this then! This bit's even better. My job's at a big new car works they've built in that new town. They'll help us to get a house, love! We're moving into a new house!

Mum: John! With a garden? and inside lav? Will it have central heating? . . .

Dad: Hey ... hold on a bit ... I don't even know myself yet ... I only heard half-an-hour ago ...

3 Narration

Carol: [*Narrating*] And that was that. Mum was dancing about as if Dad had given her a present, and he was laughing and shouting like I hadn't seen him do for years. They never even asked me how I felt about it. Moving from Woodbine Terrace. Just like that. They didn't even care how I felt. When my sisters came home from work they felt just like I did. Leave big, noisy Liverpool to go and live out in the country! They wouldn't hear of it. They had jobs and boyfriends in the city – they weren't going to leave them behind! They told Mum they were going to get a flat in town and share it. I saw my chance ...

4 The family's house

Carol: Mum, let me stay with them! Please Mum! I'll do anything! I'll come out every weekend to see you and Dad!

Mum: Don't talk daft. You've not left school yet ...

Carol: Let me stay here then, at Zena's. I know her Mum would have me ... just till I finish at school. Please Mum, let me! Don't make me leave Liverpool!

Dad: You must be mad, girl. Do you know what a chance like this means? Away from all this noise and dirt and everyone on top of everyone else? You won't know yourself, out in the country.

Mum: Carol, you're being silly.

Carol: I don't want to go ... I don't want to leave the terrace ...

Mum: Is this what it's going to mean, John? Breaking up a family?

Dad: You mustn't look at it like that love. Our Dave will be with us, and our Carol too, whether she likes it or not. And Shirley and Joan . . . well . . . they're of an age now to be leaving home. We've got ourselves to think of now. Our own future.

5   Narration

Carol: [*Narrating*] I was too upset to say anything. I sat staring out of the window and my mate Zena came out of her house and started pulling faces at me . . . did I want to go down to the chippie with her? I just shook my head, miserable. I was leaving the terrace. That was all I could think about. We moved six weeks later. I remember how hot it was that day. I remember sitting on the grass verge outside our new house with our Dave, watching some kid wobbling up and down the road on his bike. You'd think he owned the place. I could hear Mum and Dad's voices drifting out through the open window, as they were sorting out the furniture. Mum was that excited.

6   At the new house

We hear children playing, the sound of bikes and birdsong.

Mum: Just look at the size of this living-room! We could fit the whole of our other house in here.

Dad: It's going to be a problem furnishing the place.

Mum: D'you know, I feel as if I want to chuck out all this stuff of ours. Just dump it somewhere. Wouldn't it be lovely to start fresh?

Dad: It'd be lovely to have enough money! You never know, you might pick yourself a little job up somewhere round here.

Mum: I'd love that! I could manage, couldn't I, now the other two are off my hands . . . and our Dave's going to be at school all day. It's going to be a real new beginning for us, John. For both of us.

7 Narration

Carol: [*Narrating*] And she never stopped. Day after day she was more and more full of herself.

8 At the new house

We hear birdsong and voices.

Mum: Carol, come and give me a hand with these sheets, will you? It's nice to know they'll come back in as clean as they go out, that's one thing! Just smell that air! I feel as if I can taste it! I feel as if I could swallow up the sunshine.

Carol: I hate it. It's too quiet.

Mum: Quiet! With all those birds shouting about! Just listen to them. There's different things to listen to here . . . no cars, no screaming kids . . . and look at our beautiful hills.

Carol: And I hate those prissy little gardens. Like bald heads with little tufts of hair growing out. I wish we could go back, Mum!

Mum: I don't know what's up with you. You've done nothing but mope since you came here. You don't think Zena's going round moping for you, do you?

Carol: It's not just Zena . . . it's everyone. It's the terrace. Don't you miss them? All the neighbours popping in?

Mum: I do not. They respect your privacy here . . . keeping themselves to themselves instead of living everyone's life for them. It makes a change to be able to sneeze in your own front room without someone next door shouting 'Bless you!' Right, that's them done. I'm just popping down to the club for five minutes. Come on down for a bit, Carol . . . there might be someone of your age down there . . .

9   Narration

Carol: [*Narrating*] That was another thing. The club. I hated that club. Mum was there all the time. She'd got herself on the committee. She might as well have gone and lived there. All she could talk about was the soft-piled carpet in the concert room, and the swirly blue curtains, and the fabric seats on the chairs. They were going to have the official opening at the end of the month. There was to be a kids' party in the afternoon, and a dance and cabaret in the evening. She was always on about it, every minute of the day . . .

10   At the new house: the kitchen

We hear **Mum** *washing up.*

Mum: We've found a magician for the kids party . . . do you know, he lives just round the corner! Just imagine! He breeds rabbits . . . you know . . . the little fellow with the teeth. That's him! Oh, Carol, I've put you down for pass the parcel . . . now *what* we're going to have for the cold buffet, I don't know . . .

11 Narrating

Carol: [*Narrating*] On and on and on . . . Dad was thrilled to bits with his job, and having money to spare to pop out for a drink, and he loved to see Mum looking so happy. No one noticed how miserable I was. No one cared. Nobody cared how much I hated the place. All they could talk about was the Social Club, the Social Club, and its blessed all-important opening night. I hated it. It had taken my Mum right away from me. She didn't care. I hated the place. I wanted to go home. Then, the day before the club was due to open, Mum and I both got letters in the post. Mine was from Zena! I hadn't heard from her for weeks! She wanted to meet me in town . . .

12 At the new house: the kitchen

We hear the sound of food frying and cutlery.

Carol: Mum . . . I'm going into town tomorrow.

Mum: Well! Look at this! John!

Carol: Can I, Mum – just for the day?

Mum: Just a minute, love.

Carol: Can I?

Mum: What?

Carol: Go on Saturday . . .

Mum: Go where? You're going nowhere on Saturday! It's CLUB day! Club opening day! We're going to need all the help we can get.

Carol: Mum . . .

Mum: Read this John . . .

Carol: Please . . .

Mum: No! I've told you.

Dad: What's this then?

Mum: It's from the club. What d'you think of that?

Dad: Hey, this is marvellous! Have you seen this, Carol? This is good news!

Carol: Don't tell me. We're moving. I've heard that one before. Sunday then? Can I go Sunday?

Dad: Your mother's been offered a job. She's been put in charge of catering.

Mum: At the club! At my club! Starting from tomorrow. You'll have to cook your Dad's Sunday roast, Carol. That'll be your job now.

Dad: Come on, Carol, what'yer looking so long-faced for now? What do you say to your mother?

Carol: I'm sick to death of hearing about that flamin' club! It's like waiting for someone's baby to be born, the way you all go on about it. I hate it! You're never here – you're always either talking about the place or going round there. And now you're cooking there as well. It's us you should be cooking for, not them! What did we have to come here for anyway? I hate it here. [*Going out*] I hate this house and I hate this silly plastic town and I hate that bloody club!

Dad: [*Shouting*] Just you come back here, Carol. What the hell's up with you? . . . Come back here . . .

Mum: Leave her John. She'll get over it. She'll love that place when she sees it. She'll never be out of the place, you'll see . . .

13   Narration

Carol: [*Narrating*] I heard that all right. It was as if someone had pushed a great heavy door between us and the old life. The terrace. I wanted to go home. This place wasn't home. I ran off down the road, past the houses and shops to the club. I could see the trimmings inside it; all the chairs and tables neatly laid; the mirror ball catching the street lights. All set up for tomorrow. I knew exactly what I was doing. I can remember the sound of someone sobbing, and I realised that it was me I could hear – just as the girl I was watching in the long dark window was me. I saw the girl take the stone and fling it against the window. She brought matches from her pocket and the sharp flare lit up her face so that she and I, my reflection and me, looked at each other for a second. The match touched the swirly blue curtains that my mum had described so often. More matches, like tiny bright arrows, darted through onto the soft-piled carpet and onto the fabric seats of the chairs below. I could hear my mum's voice . . .

[**Carol** *imagines her parents talking*]

Mum: Beautiful, it is. All wood and fabric. One match would set the whole place alight.

Dad: No love, they'll have treated it. They don't take chances like that. Not the way people are these days.

Carol: [*Narrating*] But what they did forget to treat were the festoons of paper chains that looped across the ceiling like spiders' webs, trailing in fringes down the pine walls. One of my matches caught a strand. The flare shot across the ceiling. The flames were like licking tongues, eating along the buntings. The paper curled and flickered and drifted down like stars. I couldn't keep my eyes off them.

Carol: Quickly I lit another match, shoved it in the box with the rest, and threw it as far as I could through the window. Black smoke came curling through. Suddenly I was more frightened than I'd ever been in my life. I ran and ran as though the flames were eating up the ground behind me. I didn't dare look back. I hitched a lift into Liverpool. I walked till my knees felt like knots and my feet were burning. It was growing light when I reached Woodbine Terrace. My head was bursting with little explosions like matches striking, but I was happy. I'd destroyed the thing I hated. I was home.

14   Woodbine Terrace: outside the old house

We can hear noises in the distance: a pneumatic drill.

Carol: Oh! Oh no! What have they done! Someone's broken all the windows. Like great black eyes staring out at me. And they've kicked down the door! ... smashed it in ... I can't get past! What have they done? The floorboards ... and the skirting boards ... they've even pulled out the rotten old fireplace. It's nothing but a heap of rubble ...

[*We start to hear noises of burning*]

Carol: [*Narrating*] I cried myself to sleep, there among all the debris of our old house. I dreamt about a huge furnace, with the flames leaping so high that even birds' wings caught fire. Great girders splintering and walls crumbling into it like sand. And my mum, screaming, running into the flames, looking for me.

15   Inside the old house: early morning

Mum: Carol! Carol!

[*The sounds of burning fade and we hear a milk float in the distance*]

Carol: Mum! I'm here! I'm here! Mum!

Mum: All right love. You're all right now. Come on pet. We've come to take you home.

Dad: We've come to show you the mess you've made of that bloody club!

Mum: Leave her, John. The kid's upset. Just leave her. Come on, our Carol. Let's get you home.

16   Narration

Carol: [*Narrating*] She was great, my mum. She never said a word about what I'd done to her club. Oh, they took me there all right, and a policeman interviewed me and then they showed me what I'd done to the concert hall – all scorch marks across the ceiling and the walls and the pile carpet ... the curtains all frizzled up ... the chairs all pocked ... broken glass everywhere. It looked terrible. My Dad was too angry to speak. Mum was white and tense – but she kept her hand on my arm all the time ... sort of reassuring me. She never said a word. We walked back to the house in silence, the three of us, and then Mum gave Dad a meaningful look.

17   Back at the new house

Dad: We've been talking it over, your mother and me. I don't understand what made you do this ... a terrible thing like this, Carol, but you've made your point. If you want to go ... you can go. We've spoken to your sisters about it, and you can make your home with them. But we're not leaving. Our future is here. We're staying.

Carol: I looked over to Mum. She didn't say a word. She was just staring at Dad, to make sure he said it the way she wanted it said. I went and stood by the window. Our Dave was watering the border plants Dad had put in the daft little garden. There were some kids playing out in the road, the sun was settling onto the hills, and across the rooves of the tidy houses.

Carol: Mum. Dad. If it's all right with you . . . I think I'd like to stay.

Grandma Goes West
Michael McStay

*First broadcast on BBC Radio 4 on 19 February 1983 (directed
by Jane Morgan)*

Characters

Sid
Sadie, his wife
Stanley ⎱
Sophie ⎰ their children
Grandma, Sadie's mother
Terry, a friend of Sid's
Policeman
Doctor

Grandma Goes West

---

1 The local pub: just after opening time

We hear the general muted chatter of the pub. **Terry** *is at the bar and spots* **Sid** *entering.*

Terry: [*Calls*] Evenin' Sid! Over here!

Sid: [*Approaching*] Hullo, Terry, my lad! How's it going?

Terry: Oh, fair to worse, you know. I'll buy you a pint.

Sid: Oh, ta!

Terry: Sally! Give us another pint will you love? [*To* **Sid**] So . . . how was your holiday?

Sid: Don't ask me! Haven't I told you?

Terry: I haven't seen you.

Sid: Oh, well – wait till I tell you! The mother-in-law died.

Terry: You wha'? That's dreadful.

Sid: Yeah!

Terry: Poor Sadie! Here – have a sup of that.

Sid: Oh, cheers! So – I thought we'd leave early in the morning to –

Terry: [*Interrupting*] Hang on! I saw your Sadie the other day. She didn't say anything. You're having me on. This is another of your stories, isn't it?

Sid: Have I ever lied to you?

Terry: I'm not going to believe a word of this.

Sid: No, no . . . wait . . .

Terry: I think I'll go and chat to Harry.

Sid: You can't leave now – it's my round next.

Terry: Well . . . you've got a point. . . .

2   A suburban street somewhere in the Midlands: the middle of the night

Sid *and* **Sadie** *are making the final adjustments to loading up the car prior to the family holiday.*

Sid: Is that everything?

Sadie: Yes. Except for the picnic basket.

Sid: What do we want a picnic basket for?

Sadie: Picnics.

Sid: We're not having any picnics. We'll be stopping off at pubs for a pint and a pastie. We're going to Cornwall, aren't we? Great for pasties!

Sadie: We can't take the children into pubs. We'll have to sit outside.

Sid: You have to sit outside with picnics.

Sadie: [*There is a pause while* **Sadie** *accepts the logic of this*] It was a present. I've never used it.

Sid: From your mother!

Sadie: That's got nothing to do with it.

Sid: Yes it has. If anybody else had bought it we could have given it to the nearest jumble sale, where it belongs.

Sadie: You try and be nice to mother. It's her holiday as well.

Sid: Don't worry! I'll be nice to her. I don't want her putting a spell on me do I?

Sadie: Sidney!

Sid: But I'm still not taking that picnic basket. Just some sandwiches and a thermos. What do *you* want?

[*Twelve year old* **Stanley** *has arrived and reluctantly approaches the car*]

Stanley: Sophie feels sick. She's eaten all them munch-mallow things.

Sid: Wait on! What's all that?

Grandma: [*Approaching*] Are we all ready to go then? Let me get into the car. I don't want to catch my death of cold out here. A silly time to be starting a holiday.

Sid: Hang on a minute! I said, what's all that?

Sadie: I feel sick, Mum.

Sid: Shut up! Is that her luggage?

Grandma: Who's 'her'? Who does he mean by 'her'?

Sid: I mean you, Grandma!

Grandma: Does he think I'm not here?

Sid: She's not taking that! Did you take all that with you on the Titanic?

Sadie: Now just calm down, Sidney. We'll just have to rethink it a bit. We'll have to leave something behind.

Sid: Her!

Grandma: Who does he mean by 'her'?

Sadie: We'll take a few things out, and then re-pack the car.

Sid: That'll take hours!

Grandma: I always said it was a silly time to be starting a holiday!

Sid: [*He starts to heave at the suitcases*] Aston Villa! I'm not going! I'm never going through all this again. Next time – you can go on holiday and leave me in the pub. Aston Villa!

3 Inside the car: the journey has begun

Sid: No Stanley, you can not!

Stanley: Oh, Dad!

Sid: I cannot stand all that 'Yeah! Yeah! Bee bop a lulu' stuff.

Sophie: But it's not that, Dad. That's Radio One. We want Radio Two.

Sid: I can't cope with that racket and the traffic.

Grandma: Music all hours of the night! People should be in bed.

Sadie: Some people work shift-work, Grandma.

Grandma: And some people are setting off on holiday.

Sid: Aston Villa! She's off!

Grandma: I heard that!

Sid: I wanted to leave two hours ago.

Grandma: Still the middle of the night. A stupid time to set off on a holiday. I always said.

Sid: Would somebody please explain to her –

Grandma: Who does he mean by 'her'?

Sid: Grandma, listen to me while I tell you once again. Is your deaf-aid turned up?

Sadie: Sidney!

Grandma: I am not deaf! I can hear every word you say. You'll be sorry when I'm gone!

Sadie: Now, Grandma! Sidney doesn't mean it!

Sid: I didn't know you'd planned on going!

Grandma: There's nothing for him in my will, you know.

Sadie: Now, that's all silly talk, Mummy. And you, Sidney!

Sid: I just want her to understand, once and for all, that I wanted to leave at this time of night to avoid the traffic.

Grandma: What would happen if everybody else thought the same way?

Sid: Well, they haven't, have they? As you can see – not another car in sight.

Stanley: Can we have the radio on, then?

Sid: Shut up!

Sadie: Sidney!

Sid: I want you all to try and get some sleep. In six hours time we shall be in Mousehole ...

Sophie: Mowzel.

Sid: What?

Sophie: Mowzel. That's how it's pronounced.

Sid: What are you talking about?

Sophie: It's spelt Mousehole, but they call it 'Mowzel'.

Sid: Do they! Bloody silly!

Sadie: Now, Sidney!

Sid: Anyway, that's where we shall be in six hours time. So, it would be a good idea –

Grandma: I'm not sitting for six hours with this picnic basket under my feet.

Sadie: Sidney! You've never put that picnic basket under Grandma's feet!

Sid: Well, where else? I couldn't put it under my feet, could I?

Grandma: I'm nearly crippled now.

Sadie: But why didn't you say earlier?

Grandma: I've never been one to complain, Sadie, love.

[**Sid** *makes an explosive noise*]

Sadie: Well, give it over to me. No! Don't you struggle with it. Stanley, give a hand!

Stanley: I can't. [*Struggling*] I can't move it unless you push the seat-back forward.

Sadie: You'll have to stop the car.

Sid: I am not stopping the car.

Sadie: Be reasonable, Sidney.

Sid: I am being perfectly reasonable. If I stop the car we shall be half an hour while I unpack the back seat and get her sorted out. I've already lost two hours thanks to her. I'm not losing any more.

Sophie: Mum! Can you stop Stanley bouncing about? He's making me feel sick again.

Sid: You are not going to be sick, Sophie. I won't have it! I shall stop at the next Service Station where we shall have a co-ordinated 'pee' break. You can then use the time to be sick, if you so wish. I am just not going to have unilateral 'peeing' and freelance vomiting on this trip or we'll never get anywhere.

Sadie: You are being quite ridiculous, Sidney!

Sid: No I am not! However, I am prepared to use the same stop to move the picnic basket from under your mother and shove it somewhere else.

Grandma: I can't wait that long. It's giving me the cramp now. And I shall go to the toilet when I please.

Sadie: Of course you will, Grandma. He's only teasing.

Sid: I am not!

Grandma: You'll be old yourself one day.

Sid: Not if I have any more holidays like this!

Sadie: Now – Stanley, you slide over to sit behind me and let Grandma sit in the middle.

Stanley: That's not fair! It's easier for Sophie.

Sadie: Yes, but there's more room for your long legs behind me.

Stanley: Not with the picnic basket there, there isn't.

Sid: Do as you're told!

Sadie: Now, Sophie, you slide under Stanley . . . Ease over, Stanley . . . There we are! Now, Grandma . . . carefully . . . you slide along in the middle. Ease up, Stanley.

Grandma: I've got my leg stuck down the side of the basket.

Stanley: It's easier to stay like we are, Mum.

Sadie: I'm sure you're right, Stanley. But since your Father refuses to stop . . . Just ease your leg out, Mummy. Now . . . Stanley . . . climb over Grandma. Gently, Stanley!

Grandma: My leg!

Stanley: Sorry, Gran!

Grandma: It's broken! You've broken it!

Stanley: I'm sorry, Grandma! Honest!

Sadie: What's wrong, Mummy?

Grandma: I think he's broken my leg.

Sadie: Stop the car, Sidney!

Sid: She's all right!

Sadie: Mummy, are you all right?

Grandma: A fat lot he cares!

Sadie: I think you are probably all right, Mummy.

Grandma: There'll be the most awful bruise.

Sadie: Now, Mummy, are you comfortably settled?

Grandma: If these children will just keep still. Except for my leg.

Sadie: Well, everybody snuggle down for the night. We'll all try and get some sleep. And Grandma, I've got a little something here that might help.

Grandma: Oh?

Sadie: A little bottle of brandy. Have a swig of that to keep the cold out.

Grandma: You've always been a thoughtful girl, Sadie. Good to your old mother. More than I can say for him! [*She takes a large swig*]

Sid: Good grief! That's enough to stun a cow!

Grandma: Ooh! I can feel that doing me good already. I'll just have another mouthful. [*Again she swigs, and this time she chokes on it*]

Sadie: Mummy! Are you all right?

Grandma: [*Spluttering a bit*] Yes, I'm all right. I think Sidney must have hit a bump or something.

Sid: I hit nothing. You very likely swallowed the cork, as well.

Sadie: Well, you have a little drop more later. When you feel up to it.

Sophie: Can we have a sing-song?

Sadie: I'd rather you tried to get some sleep. You'll all be so tired tomorrow.

Grandma: It's a silly time to set off on a holiday.

Sophie: Just one, Mum!

Grandma: I feel like a little song!

Sadie: Mummy?

Grandma: Do we all know 'Cherry Ripe'? [*She starts singing in a high, warbling voice 'Cherry ripe, cherry ripe . . .*]

Sid: Aston Villa!

Sadie: Mummy! Mummy! Grandma! Why don't we have 'One Man Went to Mow'?

[*She starts singing this and one by one the others join in: but not Dad!*

After a while **Grandma, Sophie** *and* **Stanley** *drop off to sleep.* **Sid** *and* **Sadie** *continue talking*]

Sid: Isn't that peaceful? Now they're all asleep? The kids are bad enough, but your Mother really wears me out.

Sadie: She's old.

Sid: She hasn't improved any with age, has she?

Sadie: Oh, be fair on her! She's very fond of you, you know.

Sid: She's got a funny way of showing it.

[*We hear* **Grandma** *snorting, shuffling and groaning in the back seat*]

Sid: [*Continuing*] That's not her waking up, is it?

Sadie: No. She's still well away.

Sid: Thank Heavens for that! [*There is a pause*] We'll be off the motorway soon. Then into Cornwall and all those quiet country lanes and smashing little pubs.

Sadie: Cream teas!

[*The conversation lapses for a while*]

Sid: Your mother's stopped snoring.

Sadie: Yes. Must be awful to grow old.

Sid: I have! And it is!

Sadie: She does look funny.

Sid: Even worse than when she's awake.

Sadie: You can't see her.

Sid: I can. In the mirror. You'd better try and put her head back. Fallen forward on her chest like that she'll wake up with a crick. She'll be even more crabbie.

Sadie: Now just stop it, Sidney! [*Reaching into the back of the car*] Outch!

Sid: Now what's up?

Sadie: I think my little X has gone!

Sid: Is that all!

Sadie: I can't quite reach her. Ooh! It's sticking right in me. There! That's got her. [*There is a short pause then* **Sadie** *continues in a hushed tone*] Sidney! Sidney!

Sid: Now what?

Sadie: I don't think she's well.

Sid: What are you talking about?

Sadie: [*Hushed, so as not to wake the children*] I think she's gone!

Sid: Gone? Where? What are you talking about?

Sadie: Grandma! I think she's passed on!

Sid: Do what? Passed out, you mean!

Sadie: No! Look at her! Pull over. Stop the car!

Sid: I'm not stopping the car. It'll wake the kids.

Sadie: No, Sidney ... I mean ... Grandma ... I think she's – [*Whispering*] you know – D.E.D.

Sid: D.E.D.? Dead!

Sadie: Sidney! Shhh! You'll wake the children.

Sid: [*In a furious whisper*] Have you gone stark raving bonkers? What do you mean, saying things like that?

Sadie: Just look at her!

Sid: Yes, she looks a bit ... But, I said, she always looks dreadful!

Sadie: But, Sidney, her eyes are all open!

Sid: Oh, stop it, Sadie! She's drunk over a quarter bottle of brandy!

Sadie: And she feels, well, clammy!

Sid: Clammy?

Sadie: Cold! Awful!

Sid: Oh, pull yourself together! Give her a shake. Go on! Wake her up! You'll find out how awful she can be.

Sadie: I can't! I'm frightened!

Sid: Don't be silly! Give her a good shake!

Sadie: Oh, dear! [*She reaches back*] Ooer! It's in me again! I'll have to buy a new one! Mummy! Are you all right, Mummy? [*She gives a tiny, stifled scream*]

Sid: What's up?

Sadie: Her head! It's lolling about all over the place!

Sid: Well don't let it wake the kids. Feel her pulse!

Sadie: [*After a pause*] I can't find it!

Sid: It's in her wrist!

Sadie: I know that! I mean I can't find it. It's gone!

Sid: Well, try her heart. [*To himself*] That's no use. She's never had one of those.

Sadie: Oh, Sidney! I know it! She's gone! She must have had a seizure or something.

Sid: [*With the dawning realization*] Aston Villa!

Sadie: [*Fighting to control tears*] This is no time to be blasphemous. She is my mother, after all. Didn't we ought to see somebody?

Sid: Who? I mean, at four in the morning? Who are we liable to see?

Sadie: A doctor? Shouldn't we see a doctor?

Sid: It's a bit late for a doctor, isn't it?

Sadie: But you have to report a – loss – don't you?

Sid: How? Go on! Tell me how? I'm in the middle of nowhere. Where am I going to find a doctor?

Sadie: Yellow Pages?

Sid: I haven't got – Where am I going to find – Oh, never mind!

Sadie: We'll have to do something.

Sid: Sadie. Shut up!

Sadie: Sidney!

Sid: I can not think with you wittering on all the time. Now – please! Keep quiet!

[*There is a short silence, broken only by the occasional tearful snuffle from* **Sadie***, then*]

Sadie: Sidney?

Sid: What is it?

Sadie: What if the children wake up?

Sid: How do you mean?

Sadie: Well, it's not right, is it? I mean with Mummy like that.

Sid: She's not bothering them, is she?

Sadie: That's not what I mean. What I mean is . . . if they wake up and find her between them . . . gone. They're only children. It would be an awful shock.

Sid: Ah! Yes. Difficult.

Sadie: We'll have to move her.

Sid: Where? I'm not having her next to me. I couldn't concentrate on the driving. Not with her leering at me. It's bad enough when she's heckling from the back.

Sadie: [*With a sob*] Oh, Sidney! You shouldn't speak ill!

Sid: I'll bet wherever she is now she's giving a bad report on me. Anyway, I'm not having her in the front.

Sadie: She could sit on my lap.

Sid: Sadie! Pull yourself together!

Sadie: We've got to do something. [*The car begins to slow down*] What are you doing?

Sid: I am pulling up, Sadie.

Sid: But why?

Sid: Shh, now! [*The car stops*] Now get out as quietly as you can. Don't bang the door.

4 Outside the car: early morning

Sadie *and* **Sid** *are standing beside the car.* **Sid** *takes charge of the situation.*

Sid: I'm going to take these suitcases off the roof rack, put them on the back seat, and put Grandma up there.

Sadie: Oh! How could you? I've never heard of such a thing!

Sid: Can you think of something better? She's not going to worry, is she? And we're agreed we can't leave her where she is. And I'm not unpacking the boot again.

Sadie: What will people say?

Sid: Who are you going to tell?

Sadie: People will notice. You can't just drive around with a . . . with . . . well, with your mother on the roof rack.

Sid: Sadie, don't be silly! There's a tarpaulin over the cases. Right? I'll wrap her in that.

Sadie: The tarpaulin?

Sid: Don't worry, it won't come to any harm. Now . . . you must give me a hand.

Sadie: [*Plaintively*] Sidney!

Sid: [*Ignoring her*] If I pull the driving seat forward we can get her out without disturbing the kids. Just don't think about it. Imagine it's a sack of potatoes or something.

Sadie: I shall never speak to you again, Sidney Smith!

Sid: Good! Because we must not disturb the children. Now then, I'll start by getting these cases down. [*He strains to reach up*] This is the last time, Sadie. Never again.

5   Inside the car: the journey continues

Sadie: [*After a pause*] It's not right, you know. I mean, up there like that. She could catch her death – ooh!

Sid: Stop going on, there's a love.

Sadie: But you know what I mean?

Sid: No, I don't. There's nothing we can do for her now. And she's probably more comfortable stretched out like that, than cooped up in the back. I wish I'd thought of that when we set off in the first place.

Sadie: Sidney – you are despicable!

Sid: I'm sorry. But we've got to make the best of it. We must try not to let it spoil the holiday.

Sadie: There'll have to be a funeral!

Sid: Yes ... but not right away. You're not thinking of cutting the holiday short, are you?

Sadie: Of course we must!

Sid: But – I know! We could have a quiet little 'do' down in Mousehole, or whatever it's called.

Sadie: I shall not discuss this any further! Mummy is going to be seen off properly, amongst her own friends. Why, they'd never forgive us! You know how they look forward to that sort of thing.

Sid: Yes! [*There is a pause*] Well, how about if we arrange to have her shipped back in an ambulance or something? Maybe a train? An 'awayday' or whatever? Then they could keep her on ice until we got home? I mean, there's the kids to think of. It's their holiday, too.

Sadie: I am not discussing it. [*After a grim silence*] I think it's illegal.

Sid: What is?

Sadie: Carrying a ... a departed person across county borders.

Sid: What are you talking about?

Sadie: I've read it somewhere. Across county borders.

Sid: That's in America, Sadie. And it only has to do with minors.

Sadie: Dead miners?

Sid: Aston Villa! Young people! People under age!

Sadie: Dead children?

Sid: Oh, heckie! Never mind! Just let me get on with the driving.

Sadie: Well you've got to report it. I know that! You've got to report a ... a departure. You can't just go careering off around the country. Carrying departed people all over the place. That's illegal. I know that.

Sid: You might be right.

Sadie: I am!

Sid: Right! Right!

Sadie: What are you going to do?

Sid: Leave it to me. Just leave it to me. [*After a short pause*] There! Over there.

Sadie: What?

Sid: A light. A house. Maybe a farm. Somebody's up.

Sadie: What are you going to do?

Sid: [*The car draws to a halt*] Report your mother. I shall go over there and use their phone.

Sadie: You're not leaving me behind. Not with – Not alone at this time of night. In the middle of nowhere.

Sid: It'll soon be getting light. But never mind. Suit yourself.

Sadie: And the children. We can't leave them here.

Sid: Then we'll all go. Wake 'em up. I'll be back in a moment. [*He gets out of the car*]

Sadie: Sophie! Sophie, wake up, love.

Sophie: [*Sleepily*] What is it, Mum? Are we there?

Sadie: Not yet. And you, Stanley. Ouch!

Sophie: What's the matter, Mum?

Sadie: Nothing. It's all right. It's my little X. Stanley? Are you awake? Ow! I can't reach round there. Give him a shake, Sophie.

Sophie: Stan! Mum says to wake up. Stan!

Stanley: Aw! I'm stiff, Mum. What's a matter?

Sadie: We're all going for a little walk. With Daddy.

Stanley: Oh! Why? What for?

Sadie: Don't whine, Stanley! We're going to make a phone call.

Stanley: Can't you go by yourselves?

Sadie: No! We're not leaving you alone out here in the middle of nowhere. Heaven knows who might come along.

Stanley: Nobody, Mum. Not in the middle of nowhere.

Sadie: Stanley, it will do you no good at all if you try and be clever with me. You are both coming along.

Sophie: Where's Grandma?

Sadie: Er . . . she's gone.

Stanley: Where?

Sadie: Well, she's gone before.

Stanley: Couldn't she make the phone call by herself, then?

Sadie: I mean that she's no longer with us.

Sophie: Where is she then, Mum?

Sadie: I hope she is in a better place.

Sophie: But she was the one who wanted to go to Cornwall.

Sadie: You obviously do not understand, Sophie. Perhaps your father will explain. In the meantime, we will all get out of the car and find your father.

Stanley: Has he gone too?

Sadie: Just get out of the car!

[*They all do so*]

6   Outside the car

Sid: [*Approaching*] I can't find a road anywhere. But there's a track that seems to lead in the right direction.

Stanley: Dad, where's Grandma?

Sid: Up on the roof rack. Now, I've got the torch, so we'll all keep together. Don't want anybody getting lost, do we? Off we go then!

Stanley: Why don't grown-ups ever give you an honest answer?

[*The family set off along the track*]

7   Returning to the car

It is now day-break and we hear birds singing and a cock crowing.

Sid: Well, whoever heard of people not having a phone in this day and age?

Sadie: But what do we do now?

Sid: We'll just have to get back in the car and drive. We must come to a village or something soon.

Sadie: I'm hungry, Mum.

Stanley: So am I.

Sadie: Right! I suggest we have breakfast now. Now then, Daddy, where's the car?

Sid: Here!

Sadie: What do you mean?

Sid: Here!

Sadie: Stop saying 'Here', Sidney! Where is it?

Sid: It's gone!

Sadie: Gone?

Sid: Gone!

Sadie: What do you mean, 'Gone'?

Sid: Gone! Not here! Vanished!

Sadie: I don't understand you, Sidney! Where is it, then?

Sid: I don't know, do I? I left it here.

Sadie: Do you mean it's gone?

Sid: Yes! Gone.

Sadie: This can't be the place.

Sid: Sadie, this is the place all right. There's the broken litter bin. There's the rusty bike. And there's the track we have just been down. No doubt about it.

Sadie: But ... what about breakfast?

Sid: Bugger breakfast! What about Grandma!

Sadie: [*With a wail*] Ooh, Sidney!

Sophie: You said Grandma had gone.

Sid: She has now!

Sophie: But if she'd already gone –

Stanley: Where was she, then?

Sid: Up on the roof rack.

Stanley: [*Not believing him*] Oh, Dad!

Sadie: What are we going to do, Sidney?

Sid: Think! I've got to think! things aren't too bad. Everything in the car was insured.

Sadie: Sidney!

Sid: Don't tell me you haven't paid the policy?

Sadie: Think of Grandma!

Sid: I am doing. I can only think of 'Household Contents'.

I mean, you can't claim her under 'Freezer Breakdown', can you?

Sadie: Sidney Smith, you are being deliberately hurtful. Once this holiday is over –

Sid: Sadie, my love, of course I'm worried. But I cannot think while you are continually having hysterics.

Stanley: Dad, is 'up on the roof rack' like 'Aston Villa?'

Sid: [*Absently*] What?

Stanley: You know, when you don't want us to hear you say 'Jes –'

Sadie: [*Interrupting very hastily*] Stanley!

Stanley: But you know what I mean? So instead of saying that, he says 'Aston Villa'. Is 'Up on the roof rack' the same sort of thing?

Sid: I don't know what you are blathering about! Now, we have no alternative but to walk to the nearest village. So, we'll put out best foot forward. Single file. I'll go first, and Stanley can bring up the rear. [*Leaving*] Keep your eyes peeled for pirates, Stanley!

Stanley: [*Leaving*] What's he talking about pirates for, Soph? I think he's flipped, you know?

8 Inside a small police station

Policeman: I see, sir. Not always a good thing to leave everything in the car. Registration Document, Licence, etc.

Sid: It seemed the safest place.

Policeman: Not if you then proceed to lose the car.

Sid: Officer, I didn't intend to lose the car. I only left it to make a phone call.

Policeman: Failing to lock the car door, and leaving the key in the ignition.

Sid: I admit that I have been thoughtless.

Policeman: Just so, sir. I feel that you must shoulder some considerable burden of the blame, in that case. For every criminal act there is often an act of equally criminal negligence.

Sid: You mean, for every unmarried mother there is an unmarried father?

Policeman: Exactly, sir! The very point I am trying to make!

Sid: Aston Villa! Are you going to bother to try and find it then?

Policeman: The wheels of justice have already been set in motion. You may have noticed me pass a slip of paper to the young lad in the next office? Within moments, every police station in the county had been notified, and every officer alerted to the crime. The first of the day, by the way. Which means there is a very good chance of having your car spotted before their notebooks get clogged with details of missing cats, runaway horses, and stolen grandmothers.

Sid: Stolen grandmothers?

Policeman: Sir?

Sid: Nothing! Nothing at all! What made you say that?

Policeman: What?

Sid: Stolen grandmothers?

Policeman: A turn of phrase, as you might say. Now, don't tell me you want to report a stolen grandmother as well? [*He gives a little laugh*]

Sid: No! No! Goodness me, no!

Policeman: Are you all right, sir? I mean, you look a little pale.

Sid: I'm fine. Really. I mean, I've been up all night. Driving, you know. And then the car . . . it's all been a strain.

Policeman: Of course, sir! I have been remiss, chatting like this. Why don't you rejoin your wife and family next door, and I'll see to it that you get a nice, hot cup of tea.

9   A waiting room at the police station

Sadie: You should have told him!

Sid: Told him! Oh, yes! Excuse me, officer, I want to report a stolen car. The usual sort of thing. Contents . . . your average holiday gear for a family of four. About twenty suitcases! No, that's all. Oh! I nearly forgot! Silly me! On the roof rack, wrapped in a tarpaulin –

Sadie: Sidney! Les enfants, s'il vous plaît!

Sid: Eh?

Sadie: The children, dearest. Remember the children.

[*The door to the waiting room opens and a* **Policeman** *enters*]

Policeman: News, Mr Smith! We have recovered your car.

Sadie: Oh, how wonderful!

Sid: That was quick!

Policeman: Yes, sir. I would permit myself some small glow of satisfaction at such a speedy solution, were it not for one or two qualifying circumstances.

Sid: Circumstances?

Policeman: Circumstances, Mr Smith. It appears that two young lads, recovering from a night on the spree and finding themselves many miles from home, took the liberty of borrowing your car in order to facilitate their journey. They repented of their folly having made an investigation of the contents of the car. And of the roof rack –

Sid: Ah! The roof rack!

Policeman: The roof rack, sir. The two young lads in question gave themselves up to the nearest police station in a state of some considerable agitation, not to say sheer bloody panic!

Sadie: Oh, Sidney!

Sid: Aston Villa!

Policeman: I will arrange transport for you all to the hospital in Truro –

Sid: Hospital?

Policeman: That's right, 'Hospital'. However, before that I would like to enquire into one or two seeming gaps in your memory. Mr Smith, it seems to me that you have some explaining to do.

10   A hospital ward

Sidney *and* **Sadie** *are talking with a* **Doctor**.

Sid: Insulin coma?

Doctor: That's correct, Mr Smith. Your mother has been a very lucky woman.

Sadie: But we thought she was ... well, you know ...

Doctor: To the inexperienced person, a patient suffering from such a condition, having lapsed into a coma, would betray symptoms similar to those of a state of death. Indeed, it would be very easy to mistake the one for the other.

Sadie: But we never even had any idea she was ill.

Doctor: I have talked to her own doctor. It appears she has not been feeling too well over these past few weeks, but there did not seem any reason to be too concerned. As I said, she has been very lucky, and she will certainly be under much stricter supervision in future.

Sadie: But she never said . . .

Doctor: Your mother is also a very brave lady. She did not want to worry you unnecessarily. Some elderly folk are like that. They would rather risk jeopardizing their own health than cause concern to those nearest and dearest to them. Your mother is obviously just such a woman.

Sid: Doesn't sound like your mother.

Sadie: Now, Sidney! I've always said you never really understood her.

Doctor: I must also add to her qualities the fact that she is an extremely tough old bird, if you will pardon the phrase!

Sid: There I have to agree with you.

Doctor: In view of the, er . . . somewhat unusual course of action you took. Well, I will not dwell upon that. Let us just say that she is extremely lucky, and there is no reason why she should not be with you for many years yet.

Sid: That's good!

Doctor: She would like to see you, but she is very weak and considerably shaken, so only a very brief word. And, by the way, I have not told her of the circumstances of her arrival here. If you follow me?

Sadie: Thank you, Doctor.

Doctor: Perhaps you'd like to move across to her now . . .?

[**Sadie** *and* **Sidney** *follow the* **Doctor** *to* **Grandma**'*s bed*]

Grandma: I don't understand the most of it, Sidney. I only know that I have put you to a lot of trouble.

Sadie: You don't worry your head about that, Mummy.

Grandma: But I do, Sadie. I've often misjudged Sidney in the past. And now when I realize what he has done for me . . .

Sid: Don't talk about it, Grandma.

Grandma: But I won't forget it. How you found those lads, and persuaded them to rush me to the hospital, while you went off to phone the police. And then left yourself with no car and miles to walk to the nearest village . . . Well!

Sid: Please! Don't say any more!

Grandma: Well, I won't. But I won't forget! Now they are going to keep me in here for a while, but you must promise me that you won't let that spoil your holiday. You just go off and try and have a good time even though I won't be with you. Can you manage that?

Sadie: Oh, Mummy!

Sid: We'll try, Grandma. It won't be easy, but we'll try.

11   Inside the car

The family start their holiday without **Grandma**.

Stanley: Can we have the radio on, Dad?

Sid: Why not? A bit of music to brighten up the day!

Sophie: Radio One?

Sid: Don't push your luck, Sophie! Radio Two. [*He finds the station*] Ah, this is the life, eh? The open road. Any minute now a lovely old country pub. Pints and pasties!

Sadie: Cream teas!

Sid: And above all, the knowledge that Grandma is in the best possible hands. Somebody else's!

[*The radio starts to play 'You can't chop your mother up in Massachusetts'.* **Sidney** *starts to sing along*]

12   Back in the pub

We hear the general laughter of the pub in full swing.

Terry: I don't believe a word of that! Didn't that happen to Jack Fairbrother's wife on the Costa Brava last year?

Sid: Oh, I don't know about that.

Terry: [*Puzzled*] It happened to somebody . . .

Sid: Anyway . . . listen . . . buy us another pint and I'll tell you about the time we lost our poodle in the Chinese restaurant.

Cutting Loose
Angus Graham-Campbell

*First broadcast on BBC Radio 4 on 23 April 1983 (directed by
Jeremy Mortimer)*

Characters

Stephen Campbell (aged 17)
Pam, his mother
Chris, his father
Mike ⎱
Phil ⎰ two of his friends
Policeman

Cutting Loose

---

1   The Campbells' home: the kitchen

We hear the sink being filled with water.

Steve: [*Approaching*] Lovely, Mum. That was great.

Pam: Not there – put it straight in the sink. Hey! No need to splash everything!

Steve: Sorry. I'm going now. Got to go and see Mike. I'll be back later.

  [*The water is turned off*]

Pam: Right dear. Your coat's in the hall – I've put that button on. [*Moving off*] I'm off to the Club just as soon as I've cleared. My luck's in today – I just feel it.

Steve: Hope so, Mum. [*Partly to himself*] It's time it was.

Pam: You will wrap up warm won't you? [*Approaching*] Look, Steve be a dear and pop this parcel in at the Stanleys on your way down. It's that picture your Dad's framed.

Steve: All right.

Pam: Bye, love. Have a nice time.

Steve: [*Moving off*] Hope you win.

Pam: Cheerio Steve. And don't forget to call on the Stanleys.

Steve: No. See you. [*Shutting the door*] How could I forget with this in my arms. 'I feel that my luck's in.' You stupid woman. 'Have a nice time.' Yes, I'll have a good time. You see if I don't.

2   Mike's home: the garage courtyard

We hear a motorbike roar into life and rev.

Mike: [*Having to shout while the bike is going*] Hey! Hey! Hey! – Listen to that!

Phil: That's great Mike.

Mike: I'm going to circle round. Out of my way.

Phil: Mind my bike!

Mike: There. [*The bike is switched off*] Goes like a bird. Steve said he'd be round.

Phil: When?

Mike: Should be here now.

Phil: Has he made up his mind?

Mike: Don't know. I hope so. Think of the petrol.

Phil: Do you think he'll come?

Mike: He's got to, Phil. He hasn't a choice. Sooner or later he's got to break loose.

Phil: Well, he still can't decide.

Mike: A month off with us. Sun. Camping. Women, Women – eh – Phil? Or two weeks cooped up in the north with those godawful parents, and his little old auntie watching telly all day. [*Impersonating* **Steve**] 'I want to come to Spain, Mike, I really do, but my Dad's booked a chalet on the banks of Loch Sporran and Aunt May's spent the winter brewing white heather wine.'

Steve: [*Calling out*] Mike, are you there?

Mike: He'd better talk sense. [*He revs up and rides the bike to* **Steve**] Well Steve?

Steve: What?

Mike: Have you told your dad yet that you're coming with us?

Steve: I can't hear what you're saying.

Mike: [*Approaching*] Are you coming to Spain?

Steve: I'm not sure.

Mike: [*Turning off the bike*] Oh, no! It's the whole point. You *were* going to make up your mind, tell your Dad, and then let us know. We're off in a week.

Steve: I must talk it over.

Mike: Look, you do want to come?

Steve: You know I do.

Mike: Right. For godsake just tell them.

Steve: You don't know my parents ...

Mike: I do, Steve, I do ... but it's *you* that we're asking. It's not wheelchairs, it's bikes.

Phil: Just say that you're off. Live your own life. Be yourself for a change.

Mike: Say thanks very much, Scotland's been fine, but you've hung up your kilts and you're off for a randy old time on the Med.

Phil: Maybe Morocco – dancers with jewels in their bellies, and tits like cream caramel going both ways at once.

Steve: Yeah. Yeah ... I know.

Mike: They just can't say no. Steve, you're seventeen, man. For godsake grow up.

Steve: They wouldn't say no – they'd make me feel guilty. Like I betrayed them.

Phil: God almighty.

Mike: Lend me your hanky.

Steve: They've booked it all up. Can't you see?

Mike: Not through my tears. What about women? What'll you get? A quick grope through 'Gone With The Wind' at the Kirkaldy flicks, making its debut, like you, on Scottish release. Women – girls, Steve, girls – you know – breasts, mouths, tongues – I give up – you're not normal.

Steve: [*Interrupting*] O.K. O.K. Right. I want to come. But I've not got enough money.

Mike: He's not got enough money! – nor have we.

Phil: We're going to live cheap.

Steve: I haven't enough. For petrol and that.

Phil: We'll share what we've got. We've been through all this.

Mike: I'm serious Steve . . .

Steve: Oh hell . . .

Mike: No, I'm being serious: you've got to come. Next year it'll be the same – then the next, then the next . . .

Steve: I'll talk to them, Mike.

Mike: Don't talk to them Steve. Go home and you *tell* them.

Steve: Yeah. I must go. See you then.

Phil: You tell them.

Steve: I will.

Mike: You tell them to stuff it. [*Starting the bike*]

Steve: [*Going*] Yeah. See you.

Mike: Not that he will.

   [*We hear the bike roar*]

3 The Campbells' home: the kitchen

We hear the kettle whistling.

Chris: [*Off*] Hello!

Pam: Steve is that you? Kettle's boiled. [*Taking the kettle off*] Oh, Chris love, it's you. You're home early today. All go well? I've got wonderful news. You'll never believe it.

Chris: I've finished framing those cows for the Porters. They look simply smashing. Lovely gilt frame. Victorian at least. [*Approaching*] You look really excited. What's the news?

Pam: Chris, you'll never believe it. I've won.

Chris: You've what?

Pam: At the Palace. I won the golden today.

Chris: Pam, that's wonderful. How much?

Pam: 350. Look. Twenty pound notes.

Chris: Pam, I'm so pleased. Give me a kiss.

Pam: You know, Chris, I'm going to give Stevie a present. £100 or something.

Chris: That's kind, Pam.

Pam: I thought that we'd spend the rest; pocket money for Scotland. Poor Steve's not had much: all his friends have got bikes – and Elsie's Alec's got a car.

Chris: He won't get a car for £100, love.

Pam: No – but you know what I mean. He's saved up a bit.

Chris: Do you think he's looking forward to Scotland this time?

Pam: Of course, Chris, he loves it. What makes you ask?

Chris: He's older now, Pam. Hey – 350 quid!

Pam: Of course he enjoys it.

Chris: It's just he's been so quiet. Not joined in the plans – you know what I mean.

[*We hear the door slam*]

Pam: No, he loves every minute. Of course he enjoys it . . .

Steve: [*Off*] Hi, Mum. I'm back.

Pam: [*To* **Chris**] It wouldn't be Scotland without him. You know that it wouldn't.

Steve: [*Coming in*] Hi, Dad. Mum.

Pam: Hullo Steve. Had a nice time?

Steve: Yeah. Been up to Mike's. I've something to tell you.

Chris: Yes. And your mum's got some news. Haven't you dear?

Steve: Good. Out with it then.

Pam: A little surprise. But what's yours?

Steve: No. You tell me first. What is it, Dad?

Chris: Go on, Pam.

Pam: I won today.

Steve: How much? Hey – that's great. You knew that you would.

Pam: The golden.

Steve: How much then?

Pam: 350.

Steve: 350 quid? That's great, Mum.

Pam: And I'm going to give you a present.

Steve: Me? What for?

Pam: You didn't get much for your last birthday, and you haven't been lucky with work – so your dad and I thought . . .

Chris: No, your Mum did. It's her idea . . .

Pam: We thought that – I'd like to give you this. There – go on dear – take this, as a little gift – with our love . . .

Steve: But, Mum . . .

Pam: No, you deserve it. You've been so good . . .

Steve: But it was . . . you won it. Look, these are twenty pound notes. Hey, Mum, there's a hundred quid here. I can't have all this . . .

Pam: You can get something you want – you know, clothes – or put it towards a second hand car – not a motorbike mind – a new hi-fi or something . . .

Chris: Or a holiday – though as we said – we're paying for Scotland. And that's final. We're paying the lot.

Pam: With this we can live it up. Go à la carte.

Steve: That's what I wanted to talk about, Mum. I don't know how to put it. Not now with this. Look, Mum, I can't take it.

Pam: I want you to have it, love, so there's an end.

Steve: You see, I can't come.

Pam: You can't come?

Chris: How do you mean you can't come?

Steve: I can't come to Scotland.

Chris: You've found some work have you, Steve? Can't you start after?

Steve: No, Dad. I'm going with Mike and Phil. Abroad.

[*There is a pause*]

Chris: You're what?

Steve: Going with Mike and Phil.

Pam: Where?

Steve: Abroad. Spain. Maybe Morocco.

Pam: But how?

Steve: By bike. On the back of Phil's bike.

Pam: I don't know what to say. Motorbike!

Chris: I don't think this is very kind Steve. To your mother.

Steve: I can't help it. I must go.

Pam: But you've always come. We've planned it. We've got it all planned.

Chris: Of course you can help it.

Pam: We've talked about it for weeks, love.

Steve: You have, I know – but I must get away.

Chris: But we are getting away: Loch Lomond. Glencoe. Aberdeen.

Steve: You know what I mean.

Chris: No, I don't son. I don't see what you mean.

Pam: I suppose you mean from us.

Steve: You know that's not true.

Pam: But we try to give you a good time.

Steve: I know you do. Don't make it difficult, Mum.

Pam: I'm not making it difficult. I can't stop you going. I just don't understand. That's all.

Chris: It's not very kind to your mother, Steve. She's just given you a very big present.

Steve: I didn't know she was going to – did I?

Chris: That's not very nice.

Steve: Oh, but for godsake . . .

Chris: And there's no need for that. Let's remain rational.

Steve: Right. Well, let's be rational. OK. Look. I'm seventeen. I've got friends, like it or not . . .

Pam: Steve ...

Steve: And they're going abroad. They want me to go – I want to go. So I'm going. That's rational.

Pam: But how can you afford it? You've not got enough money Steve.

[*There is a pause*]

Oh. I see.

Steve: It isn't your money! I'd decided before.

Pam: I didn't think of that, did I? You live and you learn.

Steve: I made up my mind before. I promise you. Look, have it back.

Chris: So you've been keeping it secret. I've been struggling with bookings trying to find places you've always liked – and you've been planning away with those friends of yours. I'm disappointed, Steve, we've not had those kind of secrets.

Pam: Well, if he's going to go, he's just going to go. But I don't know what to tell your aunt. You know how much she looks forward to seeing you.

Chris: I just hope I can cancel the bookings.

Steve: Oh, leave it, Dad.

Chris: Well, that's just what I can't do. Someone must plan – and plan openly too – or nothing gets done. You'll learn that yourself soon enough.

Steve: For godsake, I've only just made up my mind!

Chris: That's not what you've just said.

Pam: But you've always loved Scotland. I don't understand.

Steve: It *is* what I said! Why don't you listen!

Pam: But we've never had secrets ...

Chris: I don't mind the deposits . . .

Steve: Oh – stuff the deposits. I don't want this money. Use this. Go on.

Pam: Stephen!

Steve: Have it back. Here. Take it.

Pam: Stephen . . . a present. It wouldn't be fair.

Steve: It's all blackmail and bribes. There go on. Take it all back.

Chris: Stephen, how dare you . . . speak to your mother . . . after her kindness . . .

Steve: [*Anguished, more than angry*] Oh – for crying out loud. There it is. Take it. Take it. I'm off. [*He goes out, shutting the door*]

Pam: Chris . . .

Chris: Never mind, dear.

Pam: Chris. What's happened?

Chris: Nothing – nothing at all. He's just got excited. He won't let you down. You'll see.

[*There is a pause*]

Chris: He'll come to Scotland. When he calms down.

4   Mike's house

We hear pop music being played.

Mike: Well, Phil. That's it. Packed and ready to go.

Phil: It's a hell of a lot.

Mike: Steve said he'd be here now. Can you take any more? There's this gas for the stove.

Phil: Let's give him a ring. Yes, in here – just . . . We've got to be off or we'll not make the ferry.

[**Phil** *telephones the Campbells house*]

5   The Campbells' home

Chris *answers the phone.*

Chris: Hello. Who's that? No, he's not. He's gone out. He said he'd be with you at nine? Well, he'll be on his way, then. Yes. Well, you know what I think, but have a good time all the same . . . Yes. Too exciting for us. What? Yes, off to Scotland. Peace and quiet, you know the thing. Well, don't drive too fast. Goodbye. Have a good time. Yes, I will. Bye for now. [*He rings off*] Yes. Peace and quiet. That's the thing.

6   In the Highlands: Glencoe

We hear a stream flowing and the occasional bleating of sheep.

Pam: It's a super place, Chris. You always find grand spots to picnic.

Chris: It's all good round Glencoe. The whole place is romantic. Look at the hills. The heather's just coming.

Pam: Lovely. Have some more ham. Yes – it's beautiful, Chris. Oh, I do love the hills.

Chris: Is there some going? Yes. Makes you feel free.

Pam: Two pieces more. And a bap.

Chris: Yes, thanks. Any more coffee?

Pam: Mm.

Chris: I like them like this when they're floury on top.

Pam: What? The hills? With the heather? So do I. It's just coming out.

Chris: No love. The baps. With this sprinkling of flour. You know. On top.

Pam: Oh, yes.

[*They laugh, revealing a degree of tension by their response to this misunderstanding*]

Chris: It's just like a picture. I'd like to frame the whole thing. Take it home.

Pam: Oh – you couldn't do that. You'd destroy the romance. Think of the history. The Massacre of Glencoe. The Macdonalds, the Campbells: your ancestors, Chris. It's horrible. You can almost imagine it.

Chris: Apart from the cars.

Pam: And the people. [*There is a pause*] Chris, where's Steve gone?

Chris: Down by the road. You can see him. Down there.

Pam: What's he doing?

Chris: Nothing. Just sitting. Throwing stones at the fence posts.

Pam: I wish that he'd eat something. He used to so love the picnics. Choosing the place and all that.

Chris: He's growing up love. You've got to be patient.

Pam: Give him a shout. He might want some coffee. He ought to have something. He's hardly eaten at all.

Chris: Oh, he won't come. I'll give it a try.

Pam: It's not our fault, though, Chris?

Chris: No dear. I can promise you that. It isn't our fault. He's just in with a bad group. We did right to keep him away. Steve! Stephen!

Steve:　[*Talking to himself*] Oh shut up. Leave it alone. [*We hear the sound of a stream and splashing as* **Steve** *throws stones into it. The sheep are bleating*] Talking to sheep. [*He laughs*] Glencoe. They think I hate it. Better than beaches. Picnic at massacre rock. [*Laughing again*] Massacre. [*He savours the word*] Massacre . . . [*A sheep bleats*] Creep up in the peat smell. Darkness – dark and hot – been love-making – smell of sex – smell of blood. Holding bare blades. Not like the films: meat holds the blade, but not red to start with – white flesh, like fat, white skin – damp stone in moonlight – creep up – stone breast with dark smudges – aim at the heart. Still. Slight movement: hair moves in the wind of your breath. [*Urgently*] *Still!* Don't breathe. Don't move. Sleepers move . . . Settle – chest bare – white, bare, now! Jar wrist – jolt the wrist – pain shoots up elbow – blade twists – chips bone – caught in rib – free the knife! Free the knife! Body moving, struggling in bed, twisted blanket, opening mouth, plunge into mouth, white eyes, plunge again, plunge. Ah! No bone, wrist washed warm, fist rests on chest, blood pulsing through, blade held in stone, blade . . . crying of children: then the children: every, every, every, bastard – every mother's son. [*We hear sheep bleating.* **Steve** *laughs and throws a stone which lands with a splash in the stream*] Bloody stupid sheep. Chew, piss, run. All day. [*He laughs*]

Chris:　[*Approaching*] Steve!

Steve:　[*Talking to himself*] Oh hell. Right watch this. I'll make you run.

Chris:　Steve: I've brought you some coffee. Do you want . . . hey! What are you doing?

Steve:　Trying my aim.

Chris:　[*Urgently*] Steve! Don't!

[*We hear a cry of animal pain and running hooves*]

Steve: There!

Chris: Steve. For God's sake!

Steve: Smack on the ear.

Chris: It's going onto the road.

Steve: Made it run. [*He laughs*]

Chris: There's a car. Oh – look out!

[*We hear a loud squeal of brakes as the car skids to a halt. The sheep runs off bleating wildly. The car starts up again and moves off*]

Chris: Steve! What are you doing? You could've killed them. They only just stopped.

Steve: I meant to miss.

Chris: The car could've crashed.

Steve: It was a mistake. Is that coffee? I aimed at the post. I must've missed.

Chris: I've spilt some. What's left. Steve, what are you up to? I nearly spilt the whole lot.

Steve: Has it got sugar in?

Chris: What?

Steve: Has it got sugar in?

Chris: Two. Steve, look . . .

Steve: Ah.

Chris: Look, Stephen, you must . . .

Steve: Just how I like it. I'll come up and join you. I hope there's some food left.

Chris: [*Defeated*] We've finished the ham.

Steve: I'll go straight onto fruit. Glencoe. I'm glad we stopped here. Come on, Dad. Cheer up. Don't spoil the picnic. I'll race you up.

7   On the road

A motorbike pulls up and the engine stops.

Mike: What the hell are you doing? Why've you pulled off? I could've gone straight into you! You might've warned me. What's the matter? We can't just stop here.

Phil: I don't know. It's just died on me again.

Mike: Oh God! Not again. Your bloody bike. We'll never get there.

Phil: No worse than yours.

Mike: Where are we anyway? It's the wires on your plugs again.

Phil: No, they're OK.

Mike: But you're meant to be doing the maps. You must know where we are.

Phil: I didn't know we were going to break down. Did I? We're on the right road, I know that. That's all I know.

Mike: It's not *we've* broken down; it's *you've* broken down. It's a regular feature.

Phil: Oh, leave it alone.

Mike: Here we are stuck in the middle of nowhere being roasted alive. Steve would laugh himself silly if he could see us now. We'd better wave down a car and find out where we are.

Phil: There aren't any cars.

Mike: You ought to look after your bike. One's bound to pass. He'd laugh himself sick.

[**Phil** *attempts to start the bike but the engine stutters and dies*]

Phil: We could do with him now. Do with his cash. I can't see what's wrong. You look, if you're so clever.

[*We hear a car approaching*]

Mike: There's one coming now. I'll try to stop him.

Phil: We'll run out of money. I wish Steve had come.

Mike: He's going to stop. Yes, so do I. I don't want to pay for your bloody bike. That's for sure. Right, come on and let's hope they speak English.

8   In the Campbells' car

We hear a highland reel on the radio.

Chris: Indicate can't you! Oh dear-o-dear.

Pam: I love these old Scottish tunes. They've got so much life.

Chris: Pam, give us a wipe – we're all steaming up.

Pam: Chris, look! There's a piper – a real one – just over there.

Chris: Where?

Pam: That lay-by. We've passed him. By the hot-dogs.

Chris: No – I missed him. His pipes must be soaked.

Pam: Did you see him Steve? Steve? [*There is no reply*]

Chris: I don't hold with those pipers. They're not the real thing.

Pam: No.

Chris: Legalized begging. Like in the tubes.

Pam: And more hitchhikers dear. Foreigners too, with those flags on their packs. Germans I think. So you know where they're from.

Chris: Belgians.

Pam: I can't think why they come if they're not prepared to spend money. I can't see what they see in it . . . stuck in the rain. It doesn't make sense.

Steve: If you gave them a lift perhaps you'd find out.

Pam: It's the something for nothing that I resent.

Steve: Yes. You would.

Chris: Now Steve, don't start. Let's be rational – we haven't got room. And we're so nearly there. They'd be in and then out. It wouldn't make sense. They'd be annoyed in the long run out in the cold. It wouldn't be kind to load them in here, all their packs and their gear.

Steve: [*Talking to himself*] Yes, you're so right. You're always so right.

9   A campsite in Europe

Mike *is cooking. We hear voices and music in the distance.*

Phil: Ugh! What's this for godsake?

Mike: Spaghetti – local style. I've put in some extras. Spanish spaghetti.

Phil: It's alive. Look. It's wriggling. You can't have Spanish spaghetti.

Mike: Boiling, my son. Simmering with herbs.

Phil: At least Steve could cook.

Mike: He should have learnt to say no, before learning to cook.

Phil: Look at those Germans down there – a stove with four rings. They know how to camp. Those tents are like houses.

Mike: They look daft in those tracksuits – he said to play football, when we'd all finished, the one in the green.

They're OK to talk to, once you get talking. Except he keeps needling those French guys down there. [*There is a pause*] It was the money that did him.

Phil: How do you mean?

Mike: Steve. It was a bribe pure and simple. Pathetic, the whole bloody business. It just makes me sick.

Phil: You reckon?

Mike: Yes, of course. He went home and said he was going with us, so they gave him a hundred quid to make him feel guilty, so he couldn't say no.

Phil: That's not what he said. Is that one your mate?

Mike: Of course he wouldn't say that. Yeah, the big bloke in green.

Phil: He's having a hell of a row. He's getting really stuck in.

Mike: It's those French again. He keeps shooting for goal and hitting their tent. Look, splash in some wine.

Phil: What? In there? Are you sure?

Mike: Yeah. Vino with everything. Secret of cooking.

Phil: It's gone pink. Spaghetti shouldn't be pink.

[*The voices in the distance are raised*]

Mike: The whole thing's pathetic – a hundred pound bribe to keep him away. I told him at last what I thought. We won't see young Steve again, supposing he does live through an Aberdeen August – and very few do.

Phil: Mike, do you think we should go down? There's about six of those French guys. He's giving them hell. No – there are more of them – look – over there. It's going to get bad.

Mike: He's not on his own. See – that minibus there – that's his lot – that's German – and those guys – there – they're his mates – the ones he's been playing with. He knows what he's doing.

Phil: He's your mate. You ought to go down. Come on.

Mike: No – Phil wait. Hold on – use your head. Look over there by the hut... see... the man from the gate – he'll call the police in a flash... they know that as well... we'll wait. See what happens.

Phil: I think there'll be one hell of a fight. And it's about to begin – in about ten seconds from now.

Mike: Relax Phil. Sit down. It's the way they go on – they like to show their emotions. Here we go – take this plate: spaghetti al vino. [*Exasperated*] Look, I'll make you a bet.

Phil: Right. Before we've finished this up they'll be at each others' throats.

Mike: OK. So relax and pass me the bottle.

10 Steve's aunt's house in Aberdeen

It is early evening and **Chris** *and* **Pam** *are watching television.*

Chris: Steve – come in – look at this on the telly. It's really amazing.

Steve: What?

Pam: It's smashing pictures – salmon. Salmon jumping up stream.

Steve: What's on.

Pam: It's the salmon, Steve. Doing their jumping.

Steve: Oh.

Pam: You know, when they leap up the falls. Look!

Chris: You know when they're going up stream ...

Pam: To spawn. To get back up the burns ...

Chris: Place called Buchanty Spout. We really should go there. When they get to the falls they have to leap out of the water to get up the falls.

Steve: Oh.

Chris: Hey – look at that one! That nearly made it.

Pam: Didn't quite.

Chris: They must be so patient.

Steve: I'm going out.

Chris: It's instinct you see ...

Pam: They've no choice. They just have to go up. Some never make it.

Steve: I'm going out. Or didn't you hear?

Chris: [*In his stride*] Not now, Steve. You can't go out now. Your aunt's getting the tea.

Pam: Where Steve? Tea's in ten minutes.

Chris: You haven't got time. Go after tea.

Steve: Pittodrie.

Pam: What, love?

Steve: The football. Pittodrie. To see Aberdeen.

Chris: You can't go to football – not now. Not your first night Steve. Do think, son. Think of your aunt.

Steve: Aberdeen's playing Forest. Pre-season match. It starts in thirty-five minutes. I'll just get there in time. Tell her I'm sorry.

Pam: You can't go now, love, just like that. Auntie's got on the kippers. She's taken a great deal of trouble. There are cakes and scones and sandwiches and goodness knows what. All for you. You know they're for you.

Steve: I'll just get my coat.

Chris: Steve, you can't go. Not tonight. Go out tomorrow or some other time. Not your first night.

Steve: They're not playing tomorrow. Strangely enough.

Chris: But she's hardly seen you since you arrived – it's not polite Steve.

Steve: She shouldn't spend all the time in the kitchen. I've been here for three hours. [*He goes out*]

Pam: Chris, you must put your foot down.

Chris: It's so rude.

Pam: She'll be so upset. He can't just go out. Not like that.

Chris: I can't understand it. It's not like him in the slightest.

Pam: He's getting so strange. He's normally so sensitive to moments like this. Even when he doesn't enjoy them. You must stop him dear. [**Steve** *comes back in*] Ah. Steve.

Steve: Right I'm off. See you about ten, maybe later. Don't bother to wait. Leave it unlocked.

Chris: Steve – you're not going. I'm sorry.

Steve: Sorry?

Chris: I said you're not going. You don't go to stay with someone and then go out the moment they've just cooked a meal. You're a guest, Steve. You must stay in tonight.

Pam: That's right, Steve. I know it's not easy ... with Forest and everything, but ...

Steve: I don't think you heard. I'm going out. You're the guests. You eat the kippers and watch fish jump up the telly. I'm off to the football.

Chris: You're a guest too – it's you she wants to see most.

Steve: It doesn't look very much like it.

Chris: She's busy making the tea.

Steve: Well I hope you enjoy it. I'll get a hot dog.

Chris: Stephen. You're not going out. That's final. I'm sorry. But that's how it is.

Steve: I've had enough tea. Tea till I'm sick, and enough television. And more than all that I've had enough bloody orders.

Chris: No one's ordering, Steve . . .

Pam: Look Steve . . . we *want* you to stay in – just this once. It's not much to ask. For us.

Steve: You want! God, you want this, you want that, just this once – it's not just this once – it's ten years ago and two weeks ago and ten minutes time – just this once! You want it forever. Sitting there glued to the box – so bloody self-righteous – nothing would shift you – 'Oh, don't worry dear, he'll come back, he'll be sorry tomorrow, he'll feel so ashamed he'll be quiet for a week' – oh yes, I've heard you, I know – well, we'll see. Just this once! Well, just this once we'll bloody well see! [*He goes out slamming the door violently*]

Pam: Oh Chris . . .

Chris: She'll understand. You know how much he likes Forest. Don't worry, Pam.

Pam: Do you suppose that he . . .

Chris: Don't worry, my love, don't suppose. Look, let's watch the film. Look at that one! That one got up.

Pam: I don't think it did. No, it's . . . Oh, Chris I'm so worried. He's not been the same. He shouldn't've come.

Chris: Don't worry yourself. It's a phase. Look, I know. He needs us . . . it's a difficult stage . . . it'll all work out well. He needs help . . . and our love.

Pam: I hope that you're right.

Chris: Of course I'm right, love. All will be well. I promise. Just wait and see. All's going to be well.

11 The campsite

Mike *and* **Phil** *are finishing their meal. We hear quiet pop music.*

Phil: Well, Mike – that was great. You've won your bet.

Mike: Yeah. Look at that – blood brothers again.

Phil: I couldn't move if you paid me – I'm not running about on top of that lot. I'm staying put. It's like the World Cup down there – French, Germans, Eyeties – the lot. You wouldn't believe it.

Mike: What did I tell you? All friends again – until the first foul. We'll stay here – get pissed instead.

Phil: Yeah. This is the life. All we need now are the birds.

Mike: Right. It won't be long now.

12 Steve's Aunt's house: the kitchen

The dishes are being washed up.

Pam: Well, that was a wonderful meal – and I think that's the last dish.

Chris: I feel all blown out. I've never eaten so much. And those vol-au-vents, too. [*The door bell rings*] Hello?

Pam: Oh, that must be Steve. He's back very early. Perhaps he couldn't get in.

Chris: He'll be feeling guilty, I bet. See, I told you my dear. Not a word, now. Forgive and forget.

Pam: No – I'll go. You've got wet hands. [*Calling*] Just coming!

[*The door is opened*]

Pam: [*At the door*] Oh. Hello.

Policeman: Mrs Campbell?

Chris: [*Calling*] Who is it?

Pam: Yes.

Policeman: Is Mr Campbell in?

Pam: Yes. What is it? You'd better come in.

Policeman: [*Still at the door*] I'll wait if I may.

Chris: What is it dear?

Pam: What's happened? What's the matter?

Chris: What is it dear?

Pam: Chris, it's the police.

Chris: [*Going to the door*] The police. Oh – what's up? Hello. What can I do? Are you looking for me?

Policeman: Mr Campbell?

Chris: That's right. It's not trouble, I hope. Can I help? I'm not on two yellow lines?

Pam: What's the matter? It's not Steve.

Policeman: Is Stephen Campbell your son?

Chris: What's happened? Yes, he is.

Policeman: I'm afraid there's been trouble.

Chris: What's happened? Is Stephen all right?

Pam: He's not in trouble.

Policeman: Up at the game.

Chris: What's happened?

Policeman: I'm afraid that he is. Please could you come.

Pam: He's not hurt? He hasn't been hurt?

Policeman: If you could come Mr Campbell. I'll explain. I'd bring a coat.

Chris: But what's happened?

Policeman: He's been involved in an accident.

Chris: He's all right . . . he's not . . .

Policeman: He's right enough.

Chris: Thank God . . .

Pam: What sort of incident?

Policeman: A fight, Mrs Campbell.

Chris: What? A fight? Is he hurt?

Policeman: There was a knife. There's a car just outside. I'll explain as we go.

Pam: Oh Chris . . . Steve wouldn't fight . . .

Chris: Pass me my coat, dear. I must go.

Pam: I'm coming too. I knew this would happen one day . . .

Policeman: Just Mr Campbell is best. He'll be all right, don't you worry.

Chris: You stay with your sister. I'll give you a ring.

Pam: But I want to come . . . he'll want me to come, if he's hurt.

Chris: I'll give a ring.

Pam: I knew it would happen. I knew it wasn't safe . . .

Policeman: You'll see him later. Your husband can ring. We must be off. The car's right outside.

Chris: Yes. Look. Just tell auntie I'm off to the hospital – no need to alarm her. I'll call if he needs you. All right? You're sure you're all right?

Policeman: Mr Campbell. I'm sorry. You don't understand.

Chris: What . . . ? But you said he's all right.

Policeman: He's all right. But he isn't in hospital.

Pam: Not in hospital. Thank goodness for that. For a moment I thought . . .

Chris: Then I don't understand.

Pam: Where is he then?

Policeman: He's down at the station.

Chris: The station . . . ?

Pam: Why down at the station?

Policeman: Because his was the knife. It's the other poor lad's at the hospital.

13   At the poolside

We hear the loud splash of someone leaping in a pool and a girl's laughter.

Mike: If she does that again . . . I'm soaked. Here's your beer.

Phil: Ah. That's better. Drinks by the pool. I feel like a Martini film-ad. Great. Cheers.

Mike: You're the right colour.

[*We hear more splashing and laughter*]

Mike: Right, little bitch . . . here I come!

[*He lets out a yell and there is a mighty splash*]

A Fairy Tale for Freudians

Valerie Windsor

First broadcast on BBC Radio 4 on 29 December 1979 (directed by Kay Patrick)

Characters

Storyteller
King Florizel
Queen Caroline
Vogel, the king's secretary
Mrs Orchard, an English nanny
Princess Flora, eldest daughter of the king and queen
Prince Ferdinand
Prince Adalbert
Herald
Captain

A Fairy Tale for Freudians

1 Narration

Storyteller: [*Very brisk and impatiently*] Now, I'm going to read you a fairy tale and I don't want any fidgeting. I can't abide fidgeters. If you don't like fairy tales, then you'd better practise your thirteen times table in your head. Right. [*Getting through the following details at speed*] Once upon a time in a far off country (which resembled Austria though of course it was not Austria because in this country dragons were indigenous), lived a King and Queen who had no children. [*Impatiently*] There's a lot here about frogs and pricking fingers and things . . . I'll skip all that. [*Picking up the story again*] However, one morning at breakfast . . .

2 At the castle: the breakfast room

We hear the sounds of breakfast.

Storyteller: . . . the Queen said . . .

Queen: My dear, I have some intelligence of a rather delicate nature to impart to you.

Storyteller: And the King, leaping to his feet, said . . .

King: My dear, you are not . . . ? Oh, my dear Caroline! A son and heir. You have made me the happiest of men.

Happier than the happiest of men. We shall call him . . .
Florizel . . . a thoroughly manly name!

Storyteller: [*Drily*] By an odd coincidence, as some of you
may have guessed, the King's name was also Florizel.

King: Florizel the Second!

3 Narration

Storyteller: Some seven months or so after this happy day
the Queen was brought to bed attended by seven doctors
and by the admirable Mrs Orchard. An English nanny was,
of course, de rigeur at all foreign courts.

4 The castle: outside the Queen's room

King: [*Pacing about in a state of great anxiety*] Vogel! Any
news yet, Vogel?

Vogel: [*Approaching*] I regret not, your majesty. Not yet.

King: What about the hundred gun salute, Vogel? You've
arranged it with the captain of the guard?

Vogel: Yes, your Majesty. [*Swallowing his words a little*] Or
two.

King: Certainly! Certainly you *ought* to, but the question is
have you?

Vogel: No, your majesty. Or a two gun salute.

King: [*Puzzled*] Her Majesty's dog's not dead, is it?

Vogel: No, sir.

King: Pity.

Vogel: The two gun salute, sir, is customary in the event of
the royal infant being of the female gender.

King: Nonsense, Vogel. Negative thinking. The Queen's in splendid health ... broad hips ... all her own teeth ... carefully protected from foetid air ... sinister influences ... that sort of thing ...

[*We hear a baby's cry*]

King: Vogel!

[*There is a short fanfare. The door opens and we hear a flutter of excited voices*]

King: Oh, Vogel, this is history in the making.

Mrs Orchard: [*At a slight distance*] Your Majesty ...

King: [*Beside himself*] Mrs Orchard ...

Mrs Orchard's voice: Your Majesty, it is my very pleasant duty to inform you that you are the proud father of ... [*Two loud canon shots drown her voice*]

5 Narration

Storyteller: Well, to do him justice, after the initial shock and the very natural feelings of disappointment, the king grew quite fond of his baby daughter.

6 The castle

The **King** *has recovered his composure.*

King: What name did we have in mind, my dear?

Queen: [*Tearfully*] Florizel. You were going to call him ...

King: Oh, come along, my dear. It can't be helped. We'll call the child [*Fishes about in his mind*] Flora.

7   Narration

Storyteller: Some months later, when the Princess Flora was barely crawling, the Queen sat down at the breakfast table and in a shy whisper said . . .

8   The castle: the breakfast room

Queen: My dear, I think that once again I may have intelligence of a somewhat delicate nature . . .

King: [*Excessive pleasure*] Oh my dear, you are not . . . Oh, this is wonderful news. A little brother for Flora. A son and heir. We shall call him Siegfried.

9   Narration

Storyteller: [*Briskly and without any of the storyteller's art*] However, seven months later . . .

10 At the castle: outside the Queen's room

We hear a baby crying.

Mrs Orchard: [*Somewhat truculently*] Your Majesty, I am extremely pleased to inform you that you are the father of . . . [*Two loud canon shots drown her voice*]

11   Narration

Storyteller: They called her Frieda. As the years went by such scenes as these were to repeat themselves almost yearly . . . with, of course, minor variations, such as . . .

12   The castle

Queen: [*Warily*] Now, I don't want yout to get excited and I don't want you to start thinking about names . . .

13   Narration

Storyteller: Or possibly . . .

14   The castle

We hear a fanfare.

King: Another girl, I suppose?

15   Narration

Storyteller: By this time Mrs Orchard had dominion over the upbringing of the Princesses Flora, Frieda, Frederika, Cuthberta, Alfreda, Ludwiga, Charlotta, Whilhelmina, Bernardine, Algernine and Thomasina. And by the time that it had become clear that Thomasina would be the last Royal child, the Princess Flora was almost eighteen and was the only one of his daughters that the King sometimes recognized by sight.

16   The castle

King: Ah, come in. Come in. You are . . . um . . . now don't tell me. Let me guess . . .

Flora: [*Bluntly*] Flora.

King: That's it! Flora. I knew it was, the moment I saw you. Well, my dear, you're looking very charming.

Flora: Father . . .

King: Yes, my dear?

Flora: Father . . . in a couple of days I shall be eighteen . . .

King: [*Playfully*] Ah! Birthday presents, eh?

Flora: In a manner of speaking.

King: [*Full of good humour*] Well, out with it. What is it you want? Jewels? Ball dresses?

Flora: [*Resolutely*] I want you officially to recognize me as your heir.

King: Ah.

Flora: After all, I am the eldest . . .

King: Yes, my dear, but you see . . .

Flora: So that by rights I ought to be the heir. But Vogel says . . .

King: [*Stopping her*] Yes, yes. Indeed. And Vogel is quite right. Of course, theoretically there is nothing to stop you coming to the throne, but . . . well, it's just not the sort of thing . . . decisions, unpleasantness, . . . it's a man's job Flora.

Flora: I'm not afraid of hard work.

King: Ah, yes, you say that now. From a position of comfort and privilege, but when all the cares of state are on your shoulders . . . It's not much fun, you know, Flora. There's precious little fun in being a king. And then, of course, there's the matter of slaying the dragon. There's no side stepping that one . . .

Flora: I'm sure I could do that.

King: [*Ignoring her*] . . . so you see all in all, taking one thing with another, Vogel and I decided some time ago that if we could find a prince of sufficient intelligence and courage . . .

Flora: [*Furiously*] You're going to marry me off!

King: Not 'off' exactly. What a vulgar expression.

Flora: You're going to marry me off to some witless prince and make him your heir!

King: If he kills the dragon. In which case . . .

Flora: . . . instead of me . . .

King: . . . he wouldn't be entirely witless.

Flora: . . . Your own daughter. By blood, your own flesh. I'm your natural heir!

King: The natural heir is he who kills the dragon.

Flora: But you can't give your whole kingdom away to a stranger.

King: No, Flora dear, he won't be a stranger. He'll be your husband.

17 Narration

Storyteller: And so the king sent forth heralds throughout the world.

[*We hear horses' hooves fading into the distance*]

18 Somewhere far from the kingdom

Herald: Hear ye! Hear ye! Any prince under the age of twenty-eight who aspires to the eventual succession to the throne of King Florizel the First, and to the hand of his eldest daughter, should present himself at the castle of the aforesaid . . .

19 At the castle

King: Good. Good. Splendid. First of all trials of strength, feats of arms, followed by the written paper. Then tea. And as a final test the riddle.

Vogel: Yes, sir.

King: Vogel, I don't quite understand the riddle. Could you just explain it to me again . . .

20   Narration

Storyteller: Well, whatever the answer to the riddle was, the Princess Flora soon discovered it. She was a fairly clever girl and had staunch allies in her sisters and Mrs Orchard. And as soon as it was clear which of the Princes had emerged victorious, she slipped into the ante room where Prince Ferdinand of Meinengruberhosen was awaiting his summons to appear before the king to answer the riddle. And having flattered him shamelessly – she told him the answer.

Prince Ferdinand: I say, this is frightfully good of you. A monkey holding a daffodil?

Flora: Yes.

Prince Ferdinand: A monkey holding a daffodil. A monkey holding a daffodil. A monkey . . .

21   At the castle: inside the throne room

Prince Ferdinand: [*Triumphantly*] My answer is this: A monkey holding a daffodil.

King: [*After a pause*] Pardon?

Prince Ferdinand: A monkey holding a daffodil, sir.

King: [*Sounding very confused*] Yes. The trouble is, you see . . . [*Giving up*] Vogel!

22   Narration

Storyteller: The Prince Ferdinand of Meinengruberhosen was sent home forthwith. So of course the whole complicated procedure had to be repeated . . . and repeated . . . and repeated, as is the way with fairy tales. And on each occasion the Princess managed to mislead the winning prince about the correct answer to the riddle . . . until there were no more princes left.

23 At the castle

Vogel: Well, no, that's not strictly accurate, your Majesty. He's here now. We've managed to persuade him to come to the palace, though I may say much against his will. He is the only prince who did not apply.

King: [*Gloomily*] Why not? Feeble minded like the rest of them?

Vogel: Perhaps you'd better see him for yourself. [**Vogel** *opens the door*] Prince Adalbert? Good heavens, he's disappeared again.

24 In the castle garden

We hear the sounds of birds singing.

Flora: [*Happily*] It's been a lovely afternoon. I wonder if they're still looking for you.

Prince Adalbert: I expect so.

Flora: Adalbert, why didn't you apply?

Prince Adalbert: I should only have failed at the very first test. Anyway, I've no ambition to be a king. And I'm certainly not going to kill any dragons. Not even for you.

Flora: If we were married, would you let me do all the ruling?

Prince Adalbert: Except in the garden. As long as I had complete control of the garden, I should let you do what you liked.

Flora: It would be fun wouldn't it? We could be very happy.

Prince Adalbert: But it won't happen.

25 Narration

Storyteller: Well, of course, the King was now at his wits' end.

26 The castle: in the King's room

Flora: Well, father, what are you going to do now?

King: Flora, I'm not quite sure that I approve of that challenging tone.

Flora: No princes left. You'll have to make me your heir.

Queen: Don't sit on your father's desk, Flora.

Flora: Won't you? So what about a compromise. Suppose I agree to marry Prince Adalbert.

[*The* **King** *and* **Vogel** *find this highly amusing*]

King: Prince Adalbert! Prince Adalbert!

Flora: And I'll kill the dragon.

[*The* **King** *and* **Vogel** *are laughing hysterically*]

King: You! Hah!

Flora: In fact . . . [*Struggling with her skirt*]

King: [*Suddenly panicking*] Flora, what are you doing? Put your skirt back on at once . . .

Flora: [*Still struggling*] In fact . . .

King: [*Horrified*] Flora. Shut your eyes, Vogel. Good God, Flora, what are you wearing?

Flora: Trousers, father.

King: [*As the* **Queen** *swoons*] Catch the Queen, Vogel! Smelling salts! Take them off at once. The girl's gone mad. [*Horrified*] No!

Flora: [*Innocently*] You said take them off.

King: I meant put your skirt back on.

Flora: I'm sorry, father, but skirts aren't suitable for killing dragons in. And I'm going to cut off my hair . . .

King: [*As the **Queen** swoons again*] Queen again, Vogel.

Flora: . . . and venture forth to kill the dragon. I shall return as your rightful heir.

King: Nonsense, Flora. You can't do it. You haven't got a sword.

Flora: [*Defiantly*] Then I'll get a sword.

King: You're not having mine.

Vogel: Or mine.

King: Quite right, Vogel. Or his. A sword is a man's most precious possession.

Flora: Somebody will give me a sword.

King: Don't you believe it.

Flora: Prince Adalbert will.

Vogel: Unfortunately his mother has confiscated his. In case he should take it into his head to kill his father.

Queen: Flora my dear, do be sensible. Girls don't have swords. That is what is called a fact of life.

27   Narration

Storyteller: But Flora was determined. That night, with the help of Mrs Orchard, she slipped out of the castle, dressed as a boy. Her first task was to equip herself with a sword. She lay by many a lake waiting for an arm clothed in white samite to appear until she began to doubt the veracity of her favourite poets.

She haunted many a churchyard searching for a sword which none but the rightful heir could move from its bed of stone. Alas, she found nothing. At last, utterly demoralized, she returned to the castle and slipping unnoticed into the nursery, sought the comfort of the faithful Mrs Orchard.

28   In the nursery

Mrs Orchard: [*Briskly*] Oh rubbish, Flora. Silly legends, that's all. Besides, I can't imagine what you think you want a sword for. Very vulnerable, you know. Suppose it snaps just when you've plunged it between the dragon's eyes. What do you do then? No, Flora, there are better weapons at your disposal. There's poison. There's magic. Now listen carefully . . .

29   Narration

Storyteller: And so, armed with all sorts of new ideas, Flora set forth on her travels again in search of the dragon. On her way, narrowly escaping detection and capture by the armies of her father who were all out looking for her, she had many hair-raising and extremely exciting adventures none of which I am going to tell you about because I haven't got time. At last, in a place of dark forests and high cliffs, she came to the dragon's cave.

30   Outside the dragon's cave

Flora: [*To herself*] Now then, Flora, this is it. Think of Nanny Orchard and the girls and the glory of your country. Everything ready? Right. [*Calling*] Come out, dragon! I am the rightful heir and I have come to kill you.

[*There is a pause*]

King: [*Mildly*] Good morning, Flora.

Flora: [*Sounding amazed*] Father! What are you doing here?

King: Waiting for you, my dear.

Flora: But you're covered in blood. What's happened?

King: I've killed the dragon, Flora.

Flora: Oh, Father, you haven't!

King: Well, of course I have. I had to. I couldn't risk you doing it. That would have made you indisputably the heir. Of course I shall give it out publicly that it was you who killed the dragon.

Flora: Why?

King: Well, my dear, one has to blame someone for its being dead. One always needs a scapegoat. And there again, publicly, I do need some sort of justification for the step which Vogel and I feel it expedient to take next. Captain!

Flora: What step?

Captain: Sir!

King: Arrest the Princess Flora.

Flora: [*Sounding amazed*] What are you doing?

King: I'm having you arrested, my dear. You're becoming something of a liability. You need time for a little quiet reflection. But that's between ourselves. As far as the world is concerned I am punishing you for having killed the dragon.

Flora: Then everybody will say I ought to be the rightful heir, because I killed the dragon.

King: But you didn't.

Flora: No, but . . .

King: [*Sounding pleased with himself*] Do you know, I think I'm getting better at riddles. I really am. No, my dear, I think it'll be safer for everybody if we lock you up. In a tower we thought. Without a door. A very high tower with only one window far too high up for you to jump from. Just for a few years. Just until you're ready to see sense.

Flora: [*As she is being taken away*] No. No ... please, Father, please ... what will Mrs Orchard say ... ?

[*We hear **Mrs Orchard's** opinion*]

Mrs Orchard's voice: It's a disgrace, your Majesty. I shall put pen to paper. I shall write to *The Times*. If the Princess Flora were a British citizen, you could expect repercussions ...

Flora: No... what will my mother say? Oh, Father, please ...

[*We hear the **Queen**'s opinion*]

The Queen's voice: Well, it's probably all for the best [*Coyly*] and you know there may yet be a happy ending. She may have all her sewing things ... a little light sewing provides excellent occupation for a young girl ... but no scissors. Remember what happened to her great aunt Rapunzel? Wouldn't it be lovely if something like that happened to Flora ... ?

Flora: [*As she is being dragged off*] No! ... please, no!

31 Narration

Storyteller: And so they all lived ever after. Freudians may conceivably find some sort of meaning in all this.

Follow-up Activities

The Fosdyke Saga

Discussion points

1 Invent ten comprehension questions for each episode to test whether another member of your group has understood what you think are the best jokes in each script.

2 Think about how you would 'cast' the plays.
   (*a*) What sort of voices are required for each part?
   (*b*) What advice would you give radio actors about the ways they should read the lines of the different characters in these scripts?

3 Which details (if any) do you feel are historically realistic?

4 Do you think it callous or even cruel to joke about poverty and oppression in this way?

5 Some writers have suggested that there is a kind of moral virtue to be gained from being oppressed. What do you think is meant by this? Can you think of any novels in which a character seems 'good' simply because he or she is down-trodden?

6 The critic Robert Cushman has written that *The Fosdyke Saga* 'is a joyous explosion' of that idea. Can you explain what he means by that? Do you agree with him?

7 What other plays, novels and films do you know that portray northern life? (For example, *Coronation Street*,

Billy Liar, *Joby* and *There Is a Happy Land*.) How do they compare with and differ from *The Fosdyke Saga*?

8 What different kinds of humour can you find in the scripts? (For example, puns, humour of the unexpected, excessive exaggeration.) List examples of each type.

Writing

1 Write brief character descriptions (of approximately two hundred words each) of 'Jos', Rebecca, Victoria, Ben Ditchley and Roger Ditchley.

2 Choose a section that is more or less complete in itself (such as scenes 6 to 8 of episode one, pages 30–33) and re-tell it as a realistic short story.

3 Find recent cartoon strips of *The Fosdyke Saga* or of another newspaper cartoon serial. Write your own radio drama script based on them. (Think what sound effects you will need to indicate where it is taking place. What dialogue will you have to invent to explain the action? Try to make such dialogue as natural and convincing as possible. Avoid unnatural lines in which characters try to explain everything at once.)

4 Plan and write an episode from a 'saga' of your own invention. It might for example be a local one or perhaps a story of supposedly typical Scottish, Midlands, rural or Westminster folk.

Drama

1 In the BBC Sound Effects Library, there are such comic sounds as an angel in flight, feeble applause, a batter pudding being thrown, a man drinking a bucket of cold cocoa and a man being dragged out of a piano. Try creating and recording these or other comic sound effects.

2 Rehearse and record your own tape play.

A Case for Probation

Discussion points

1 If you had the choice, would you prefer to live near a city centre, on a housing estate away from the centre, or in the country? Give reasons for your choice.

2 Do you agree with Carol's mum (scene 8, page 58) that you like privacy?

3 If you were either of Carol's parents, would you have allowed her to live with her sisters (scene 4, page 55)?

4 Have you ever been jealous of a particular interest or hobby that another member of your family has enjoyed? Can you remember and describe how you felt?

5 Just how much damage did Carol do to the club?

6 How do her parents differ in their reactions to her act of arson?

7 Why do you think Carol decides in the last scene that she will continue to live with her parents?

8 In practice, very many more boys than girls get into trouble with the law. Why do you think this is so?

9 What do you think are the main causes of inner city crime?

10 Many magistrates claim that they really dislike 'locking people up'. Do you believe this? Explain your answer.

Writing

1 Suppose the narration for the play had not all been written from Carol's point of view. Write the 'bridging' speeches of 'think' passages that might have been spoken by:

   (a) Dad in scene 3, page 55
   (b) Mum in scene 9, page 58
   (c) Dad in scene 11, page 59
   (d) Mum in scene 16, page 63.

2 Write the account of the fire at the club that might have
   appeared in a local or evening newspaper.
3 Write a poem or short story called, 'A Job At Last'.
4 Write a description of one of the dreams that Carol
   mentions in her first speech on page 53.
5 Write the report that Carol's probation officer might
   have submitted to the magistrates at the hearing of her
   case (see below).

Improvisation
1 Improvise the discussions that:
   (*a*) Carol and her probation officer might have had
        before her case came to court;
   (*b*) the interview she must have had with the policeman
        (see scene 16, page 63);
   (*c*) her mother and father had (see scene 17, page 63).
2 In groups of four or five, improvise your own version of a
   similar story in which a family has to move for reasons
   that suit some but not all the members of that family.
3 Improvise Carol's trial. Begin by studying the following
   excerpt from a radio programme about crime and punishment. The excerpt begins by explaining how a probation
   officer first gets involved in a case:

Probation officer: We will be interviewing the person
and their family and perhaps other bodies like school, et
cetera, and establishing quite a wide picture of their
circumstances, their family background, as to why they
have chosen to offend. And by doing that we can then
start to make a recommendation to the court as the most
appropriate means of sentence.
David Self: Have you taken sides at that stage? I mean
are you on the side of the young person against the law
and so on, the whole system, or are you part of the
system?

Probation officer: I have to accept that I *am* part of the system, and I'm viewed by my clients *as* part of the system, but I *don't* take sides. I'm there to look at it from all angles and look at the needs of the individual, and not to particularly judge the right and wrongs of it. If they're found guilty by a court, I have to accept that, and the client has to accept that. But I'm not there to pass judgment.

David Self: If you're a juvenile, that is if you're under seventeen, you'll be tried by magistrates in a juvenile court. If you're seventeen or more, you'll also be tried by magistrates, and only if it's a very serious offence will you then be sent for another trial before a judge and jury. But when a magistrate is hearing a case, what does he or she do? Just sit and listen?

Magistrate: Oh no, in a juvenile court one asks a lot more questions than in an adult court, but if you're dealing with the adult young offender, then there's a lot you consider. You have reports, you listen to both sides, the prosecution and the defence, the probation officer may be there to give his or her report, you can ask if there's anything more to add, you study the reports and you ask any questions that you think might be helpful . . .

David Self: How do you come to make up your mind then in the . . .?

Magistrate: Well, you retire and you discuss it and you try and think the best way of dealing with it. If it's a first offender, well, then probation is coming, or a fine. You go through all the different sentences one can do, and as a last resort one thinks of custody.

David Self: Of course the magistrates can impose all sorts of sentences when someone is found guilty. Some are intended to punish, that is, to make the guilty person suffer. Some are intended to deter, or frighten the offender from committing that crime again. And some are intended to reform the offender. So what are these sentences? Well, first there's discharge, when a person is let off with no sentence. This may be a conditional discharge, which means that the person is let off unless he or she commits another offence during a period of up to three years. Then there is the punishment of a fine, or you may be put on probation or supervision. Probation officer Brian Walker explains these last two sentences and the difference between them.

Walker: When a young person appears before the court, if they are under the age of 17 they appear before the juvenile court. And if the court feel that they are in need of support and help, or their family are, then they would consider making a supervision order. If the person is over the age of 17 then ... and the court still feel that they're in need of help and support, then they make a probation order. But it is simply that a probation order can only be made from the age of 17 onwards. The conditions are very, very similar, that they actually have to maintain contact with their probation officer, they have to be of good behaviour, and they have to keep me informed of change of address and circumstances et cetera.

For the 'trial', you will need the following characters:

Carol, Mum, Dad, magistrates (three usually sit as a panel), probation officer, police officer (to report the facts and allegations), and perhaps one of Carol's schoolteachers.

Decide whether Carol is 16 or 17 and whether her case will therefore be heard in a juvenile or magistrates' court.

Plan the order in which people will speak and then improvise the hearing.

Your magistrates can then discuss what sentence they will give. (NB What sentence does Carol receive in the play?)

Grandma Goes West

Discussion points

1 What other 'urban legends' have you heard? (See pages 10–11.)

2 Which are 'possible'? Which do you find hardest to believe? Why?

3 How do such stories differ from jokes? Do they, for example, always have a moral?

4 Why do you think the members of the family in this play all have similar names (or at least names that begin with the same letter)?

5 Do you find the family believable?

6 The mood of the play becomes much more serious towards the end. Which would you say is the first 'serious' scene? How does the writer change the mood?

7 There are plans for the play to be produced on television. Which version, the radio or television play, do you think is likely to be the funnier? Why?

8 Many comedians tell 'mother-in-law' jokes. Why should this be? What do you find funny and what do you find objectionable in jokes about particular groups of people?

Drama

1 Improvise the scenes in which the two boys steal the car, find the body and give themselves up to the police.

2 Improvise a scene involving the five members of the family which takes place several weeks after the holiday. It begins with Grandma saying, 'Sophie, I've been thinking. That night – what really did happen?'

3 Working in pairs, compile and rehearse your own comedy 'double act'.

4 In groups, plan and improvise your own play based on an 'urban legend'.

Writing

1 Write up a scripted version of one of your improvisations. (You may be able to use a cassette recorder to help you in this task.) Edit your transcript carefully so as to keep all the best lines and to cut out any unnecessary repetitions. Add lines that would improve the script (but make sure these sound natural when spoken). Write out a final version, perhaps for another group to read or perform.

2 Write another episode in the life of the family in *Grandma Goes West*. For example, it might be about Christmas Day or a visit to a shopping centre.

3 Write the true story of a car journey you will never forget.

4 Write a radio script based on another 'urban legend'.

Cutting Loose

Discussion points

1 Do you think Steve should have gone to Spain or Scotland?

2 Is Steve selfish?

3 Are his parents selfish? Or just over-protective? Or genuinely caring? Give reasons for your choice of answer.

4 Why do Mike and Phil try to persuade Steve to go with them? Is it only for selfish reasons?

5 Why did Pam give Steve the money?

6 As you first read the play, did you predict that Steve would go with his parents?

7 Did you predict that each holiday would turn out as it did? What might have happened?

8 What do Steve's imaginings about the Massacre of Glencoe tell us about him? Do you think this is just 'a passing mood'?

9 With which of the characters do you sympathize?

10 Why is the play called *Cutting Loose*?

What Sentence . . . ?

Suppose you are a magistrate in England. What sentence would you give to each of the following young people? They have all been proved guilty and now you must decide what sentence to give.

1 A 17 year old boy who has stolen and crashed a car, causing a lot of damage to the car and to a building, but not hurting anyone. He has been in court before, twice, for stealing money.

2 An unemployed 19 year old (who has no qualifications and no hope of getting a job) who has attacked an old man and stolen just enough money for a packet of cigarettes. The old man is still in hospital as a result of the attack. The young person has never been in trouble before.

3 A football fan who broke a shop window on his way home from a match, because his team lost. He was carrying a dangerous knife.

4 Steve, in *Cutting Loose*.

Plan and improvise Steve's court hearing.
NB   Steve would presumably be prosecuted under Scottish law. As he is over 16, his case would be heard in a Sheriff's Court and not at a Children's Hearing. If you know more about the English legal system, you might however choose to imagine the case being heard before magistrates (using the information on pages 140–1).

Writing
1 Write about a time you have wanted to 'cut loose'. Did you succeed? Did it turn out as you wished? Did anyone get hurt, either physically or emotionally?
2 Describe the holiday you would like to have the year after next.

3 Write a short story about a family row over money. Try writing it from a parent's viewpoint.

4 Write the news report that might have appeared in a Scottish morning newspaper, following the incident at the football match.

5 Write a poem about one of your own bad 'moods'.

A Fairy Tale for Freudians

Projects

1 Make a list of ten details in this play which are 'typical' of fairy stories.

2 Make another list of ten details or events in this play which are quite the opposite of what you would expect from a traditional story.

3 Plan and present a *This Is Your Life* or television news programme about either the characters and events of this play, or based on the story of Cinderella.

4 Why do you think people made up fairy stories? What can you find out about them? Look for collections like those of the Brothers Grimm. Are they 'suitable' for young readers?

5 Debate the motion: 'Fairy tales are bad for children.'

6 Write Mrs Orchard's letter to *The Times* (see page 136).

7 The American humourist, James Thurber, has written a famous 'fable for our time' in which Little Red Riding Hood is not taken in by the wolf but shoots it dead with a revolver she keeps handy. Write your own modern version of a story such as 'The Frog Prince' or 'Rumpelstiltskin'.

8 Improvise or write your own version of a traditional tale but give it an unexpected ending or different emphasis. Perhaps the Sleeping Beauty did not like the prince who woke her with a kiss, or maybe the bears decided to fetch the police when they found the porridge had been eaten.

9 Make up a further episode of one of the stories. Perhaps the prince began to find Cinderella was rather boring. Alternatively you might tell a tale in which the roles are reversed. Suppose there was a kitchen lad who lived with two ugly brothers. One day his fairy godfather . . .

10 Read *Guilt and Gingerbread* by Leon Garfield (published by Viking Kestrel) in which a poor young student gains the heart of a princess (by open heart surgery).

General

1 What can be included in a radio or television play that cannot be included in a stage play? (For example, a car chase.)

2 What can be included in a radio play that cannot be included in a television play?

3 Which of the plays in this book could easily be adapted for television? And for the stage?

4 Do you like plays to be realistic? Which of the plays in this collection do you find most convincing? And which (if any) unconvincing?

5 Study the *Radio Times* for one or more weeks. How many plays are broadcast in the course of a week? On which networks? Which are adapted from novels? From stage plays? Which were specially written for radio? Which are serials? What are the durations of the different plays?

6 What do you think is a good length for a radio play?

7 What sort of plays would you like to hear on radio that are not broadcast at the moment? Write a letter to Head of BBC Radio Drama (c/o BBC, Broadcasting House, London W1A 1AA) describing the sort of plays you would enjoy listening to on radio.

8 'Who needs radio drama if they've got a television set?' What would you say in answer to that question?

Coventry University

STUDIO SCRIPTS

Series editor: David Self